THE PROPHET
OF DRY HILL

Also by David Gessner

Sick of Nature

Return of the Osprey

Under the Devil's Thumb

A Wild, Rank Place

THE PROPHET OF DRY HILL

lessons from a life in nature

David Gessner

Beacon Press
Boston

Beacon Press
Boston, Massachusetts
www.beacon.org

Beacon Press books
are published under the auspices of
the Unitarian Universalist Association of Congregations.

21 20 19 18   8 7 6 5 4 3 2 1

This book is printed on acid-free paper that meets the uncoated paper
ANSI/NISO specifications for permanence as revised in 1992.

Text design by Bob Kosturko
Composition by Wilsted & Taylor Publishing Services

Library of Congress Cataloging-in-Publication Data

Gessner, David
The prophet of Dry Hill : lessons from a life in nature / David Gessner.
p.   cm.
ISBN 978-0-8070-0598-9 (pbk. : alk. paper)
1. Natural history—Massachusetts—Cape Cod—Anecdotes.
2. Hay, John, 1915– 3. Gessner, David I. Title.

QH105.M4G47 2005
508.744'92—dc22   2005007924

"Sailing to Byzantium": Reprinted with permission of Scribner,
an imprint of Simon & Schuster Adult Publishing Group,
from The Collected Works of W. B. Yeats, Volume 1: The Poems, Revised,
edited by Richard J. Finneran (New York: Scribner, 1997).

"Mayflower": Reprinted with permission of Oxford University Press,
from Selected Poems by Conrad Aiken (New York: Oxford University Press, 2003),
originally published in Sheepfold Hill: Fifteen Poems by Conrad Aiken
(New York: Sagamore Press, 1958).

We must uncenter our minds from ourselves;
We must unhumanize our views a little, and become confident
As the rock and ocean that we were made from.

ROBINSON JEFFERS, "CARMEL POINT"

CONTENTS

I

On Dry Hill

It was on Cape Cod during fall a few years back, after the century fell but before the towers did, that I began paying a series of visits to the writer John Hay. I had it in mind to write a biography of the man, whom I had always admired from afar. That book has long since been abandoned, joining a growing mulch pile of old papers. As it happened, I also abandoned the Cape itself and am no longer the permanent resident I once imagined I would be. Stranger still, John has also now left Cape Cod, the place he long celebrated in print and the place where he lived for close to sixty years.

We didn't know we were leaving back then, of course. Another fall had swept in and brushed out the humidity and tourists, and it felt like a new beginning on Cape Cod. At the time my wife and I were living in an extraordinary place, a rental house right on the edge of land and sea. Fail to make the turn into our driveway off Stephen Phillips Road and you ended up in Cape Cod Bay. I liked to take things a step further and tell friends that I now lived at the end of the world, which was—or at least *once* was—true. The boulders in our backyard provided evidence that this beach had been at the very edge of the great glacier that scraped across the Cape; smaller rocks had been carried inland on streams of ice melt, while the larger rocks that we now called ours fell straight down when the glacier melted.

I don't know why I chose that day to start visiting John. I had known *of* John Hay my whole adult life, but I had met him only a year before, when he called me up to praise an article I'd written attacking a local trophy home. We had taken a walk to the beach together, and one of my first thoughts during our initial meeting was that his voice should not be lost. There was a kindness to that voice, and a neighboring sharpness, and the things he said confirmed something I'd long felt about the importance of nature in my own life. I wasn't searching for a mentor exactly; I was too old for that—already thirty-nine and beyond the age of apprenticeship. But during our first meeting I sensed that being with him might steady me in the unconventional choices I'd made. In a culture that valued money and fame, here was a man who had spent fifty years watching, celebrating, and saving the natural world; in a culture that made celebrity and power the highest goals, here was a quieter hero. He didn't just believe that a life rooted in the natural world was a better life; he lived that way. After we parted, I found myself jotting down everything he'd said. Though he was in his mid-eighties, his mind was still keen and his memories seemingly inexhaustible, and I wanted to record as many of his words as I could while he was still here to speak.

During the walk I mentioned that I hoped to do a few interviews with him, and he vaguely assented, but then I never followed up on it. But that fall morning I just called him out of the blue. I'm not sure why; maybe the weather was right. The cranberries had been picked and the swallows were staging and I began the day by watching northern gannets, beautiful snow-white birds, as they plunged into the surf. When I got back to the house after seeing the birds, I overcame my hesitation, or nervousness, or procrastination, or whatever it was, and dialed John's number.

"Sure—come on over," he said. "I should be done writing by noon."

Just like that.

And so a little after noon I left our house on the edge and drove over to Dry Hill. I took a right at the old Red Top cemetery and pulled up at the base of his driveway. An old, uneven chunk of wood had black letters—J. HAY—painted on sloppily, a sign that impressed me with its unpretentiousness. If the sign was plain, there was also something playful and childlike about it, like the signs in Winnie the Pooh's Hundred Acre Wood. In fact, John's own woods now totaled over fifty acres. The driveway, longer than some roads on Cape Cod, wound up the hill like a trail, and my tires crunched over acorns and sticks and brown oak leaves. I had made it about halfway when I saw John shuffling down the hill, kicking up leaves around him like the smoke of a magician's entrance. I rolled down my window.

"Well, hello," he said, laughing, as if surprised I'd shown up. "I'm just off for the mail down the hill."

He instructed me to park by the house, at the top of the hill, but when I got there, no obvious spot presented itself. I should say straight out that though I had met John once before, it was at least mildly intimidating to be directly approaching him. Like anyone who has written or thought about nature in recent years, I owe a debt of gratitude to John Hay, and he looms only a little less large over the Cape Cod literary landscape than Henry David Thoreau and Henry Beston. And so I think I even parked nervously, wanting to get it all just right. As I walked down the drive to meet him, I tried to flatten out my wrinkled shirt.

I needn't have worried. When we met again, halfway down the driveway, I noticed that John wore what I would soon come to recognize as his standard garb: loose, rumpled khakis, untucked flannel shirt, baseball cap. He was walking with a cane because of a recent fall but greeted me heartily. Despite his eighty-six years, his smile still had a good deal of wattage in it.

As we approached the house, I decided to tell him about seeing the gannets. I described looking through my binoculars and noticing that the birds had wings like giant gull's wings lightly dipped in a pot of India ink. They dove from great heights into the water, dozens of them, as if pulled into a vortex. From the shoreline I watched them circle, wings beating, searching the sea from a hundred feet up, then banking down, turning, gliding, fluid until the very moment of the dive, when they would pull their wings back and shoot into the water like feathery spears. As they dove, the sun broke through the gray and radiated in every direction, spraying outward in a wagon wheel of light.

I'd been pretty excited about the sight, and I'd also been excited by the thought of telling John Hay about it. Now, standing near the top of the driveway, I tried to describe what I had seen. John kept his head cocked slightly to one side, studying me. His dark eyebrows shot up like the horned tufts of a screech owl, and his proper chin jutted out and his blue eyes grew intense. When I was done, he turned to face me directly. His right eye wandered, but his gaze, in spite of its intensity, was good-humored, as if he were thinking, *We've got an excitable one here*. It was my first experience of being assessed by that gaze.

"You should be pleased," he said finally. "Gannets are a good-luck bird."

There was something at once warm and formal about his voice. He made a sudden plunging motion with his hand. "Did you know that after they hit the water, they tunnel down like cormorants? They can swim underwater and submerge almost seventy-five feet."

He described seeing thousands of gannets during trips to Nova Scotia and England. Though the birds could spend months without landing on shore, when they roosted and bred they crowded the offshore rocks. "Bass rock in England was covered in gannets," he said. "They turned the cliffs entirely white."

He gave me an enigmatic look, a look that might have been the result of his cataracts or might have been consciously enigmatic. I didn't know.

"I'd like to see your gannets," he said.

Before we got to the house, John reached down and plucked a bay-berry leaf, smelled it and identified it as *Myrica pensylvanica*, then jammed it under my nose. He smiled broadly and for a moment stood still, seeming to forget where we were or where we were going. But it was less a panicked forgetfulness than a delighted one. "Exaltation takes practice," he once wrote, and a lifetime of practice seemed to have paid off.

It wasn't all sweetness and light, of course.

"I was down at Gray's Beach watching terns last spring," he said to me when we reached my car. "There were these two women walk-ing down the boardwalk. All this life was swirling around them—laughing gulls, ospreys, terns—but they were not seeing it. They each had a cellular phone and they were both talking—separately!—into their phones. Now, I understand we are social creatures, but we seem to have lost the ability to be alone and to look outward. They didn't look anywhere else, just staring ahead and talking, and I thought this was a perfect metaphor for how we visit our landscapes. They were blind to it. We're all blind. That's the real trouble. We need to open our eyes."

I nodded, not quite sure how to react to the preaching—yelling "Amen!" didn't seem exactly right—and we walked the rest of the way in silence.

At the house John gestured for me to wait while he slipped inside to drop off the mail. I studied the building, which, like his clothing, was modest. In a way the house was just the opposite of the new houses that were sprouting up all over Cape Cod. The current trend was to tear down old family cottages (still universally called Cape Cods) and then build oversized condolike homes that muscled out to the edge of property lines or peered over the beaches. If these new houses could be said to have a personality, it was that of the straining overachiever. By contrast, John's house sat comfortably and humbly, almost invisibly, amid the acres of trees that covered Dry Hill.

When he came back outside, John led me up the path to his studio in the woods. "This is my commute," he said. "I've been walking it for over fifty years."

We climbed a small trail through the oak leaves to the top of an even higher hill, the highest point around, where his studio stood. Like the house, the studio was modest: a small, well-built shack with large windows facing east. Planted among oaks, pitch pines, and a few birches, it was covered with cedar shingles and topped with a roof that slanted down to the west. A red brick chimney climbed its north side.

"When we moved here, this hilltop was practically bare," he said. "You could see the bay from both the house and the studio."

He opened the studio door and we stepped inside. I took note of the desk and typewriter, the piles of manuscripts and rows of full bookshelves, and the large picture of Walt Whitman tacked to the wall. This was the place where John had written the bulk of his sixteen books, and the place he still shuffled up to daily, doggedly, despite failing eyesight and waning powers of concentration and creativity.

"There have been a lot of battles in here," he said, sighing.

There's something personal about being shown a writer's study. For all John's love of the outdoors, I wondered if this wasn't where he felt most comfortable, at least when the work was going well. "When we write, we go to a place only we can go to," said a former teacher of mine, Lucia Berlin. This was the place where only John had gone almost every day for the better part of sixty years. If the house atop Dry Hill was his retreat, here was a retreat within a retreat. No phones, no errands, no worries, nothing else allowed inside these walls (except, as I would learn later, an intercom, so his wife, Kristi, could reel him back in for lunch).

John pulled up a chair and gestured toward another with his cane. When we were both seated, with his desk between us, he slapped and then rubbed his thighs as if to say, "Let's get down to work." It made sense: the studio, after all, was the place for work. Why mess around?

"Well, you mentioned you had some questions," he said.

I did have questions, lots of them, and I pulled a list out of my pocket. Before I began, however, I asked him if I could tape our conversation on my micro cassette recorder. This was a risk, I understood, and might change the nature of our budding relationship, but I thought the risk was worth it. In his early books John had preserved the voices of old Cape Codders like Harry Alexander, the warden at the herring run, and his neighbor, the barber Nate Black, and in turn I hoped to preserve his voice. I understood that some people became flustered when facing a recorder, but John agreed readily.

As the sun shafted in through the large plate-glass window, I asked him about his personal history. He replied fluently to my questions, speaking in full sentences in the manner of someone used to lecturing, without a lot of hesitation. It didn't take much prompting to get him digging into the past, and soon I was mostly quiet. I settled into my chair and listened as he began to relate his personal history.

I already knew the basics.

John was a modest man, the furthest thing from a chest-beating self-promoter. He wasn't a celebrity, either, even in his own town, and his life had been unexciting by modern media standards. Nonetheless, his biography had ascended into local myth. Many knew the story of how he and Kristi came to Cape Cod to settle on Dry Hill in 1946, in the wake of World War II. How they had bought ten acres before the war, for twenty-five dollars an acre, on a hilltop less than a mile from the sea. And how upon his return from the army, John, searching for stability in the face of a violently unstable world, built his house on the hill, thinking he might stay a while.

As it turned out, he never left. And strangely—at least by modern standards—it was the drama of settling and wedging down into one place that fired John's imagination. "Living on the 'edge of no-where' did not cut me off but teased my spirit into the open," he wrote. "Fish, birds, trees, and the weather called for some recognition in me that I had been unwilling or too self-centered to meet." Once the recognition was met, he saw his task. Thoreau referred to himself as "the inspector of snowstorms," and John became the steward of the seasons on Cape Cod. For fifty years he fulfilled that function, stand-ing sentinel, watching the turning year. He noted the small changes: the flocks of cedar waxwings feeding on berries in winter, the peepers in spring, the water roiling with fish and feeding terns in late summer, followed by the swallows' staging, the winy smell of apples in the early fall, the bittersweet berries emerging red from their cases of yellow as winter again approached. Over the years these phenological events became so imprinted on him that they became part of his internal landscape.

I asked him how he had chosen Cape Cod, and he said it had cho-sen him. "Why did I come here?" he said, echoing my question. "What was I looking for? I suppose I came here following some vague urge for space. You have to understand that when I was a boy, the population of this country was only about 90 million—now there are 320 million of us! This town had only 800 people—a small village. As a young per-son I'd been cooped up in New York most of the time. I suppose I had a hunch that it was *space* that I was after in coming here. But it took a while to fall for this place. The Cape seemed a barren land that imag-ination had to fill out."

I wasn't sure at first what John meant by *space*. But it was clearly an important word for him, a hieroglyph that stood for more than its literal meaning.

"I was never quite certain why I came here in the first place," he said. "I wandered for a year after my discharge, and then I thought of this land. I was drawn back to it. The man who sold me this place called it a 'worthless woodlot,' and I was inclined to agree at first. It was a *dump*. The trees were like stumps. For a while I wondered what the hell I was doing here. That was the original mystery. What I really loved as a boy was New Hampshire. What I loved was *trees*, and there were no trees here to speak of."

The Cape, a young land geologically, had been settled by Europeans longer than almost any place in the country. And it is one of the basic ironies of contemporary Cape Cod that by the time John moved here in 1946, the area had been long stripped of trees, for fuel, homes, and shipbuilding, and that today, as it is being developed beyond recognition, the remaining land is covered densely with trees and brush.

I asked John when he had started to see the possibilities of Cape Cod.

"What finally redeemed it for me was the sea," he said. "Water, of course. Always moving. The whole Cape fragile and alive, moving. Being shipped away. The *sea*. It wasn't as if I'd never swum in it or been on it in a boat. It's just that I had never conceived of the sea as a home. I should have, of course. The place where all life comes from. I thought of it as a place of mystery in the adventure stories I read as a kid. But I never thought of it as a giant repository of life. Then, one late spring, I walked all the way down from Provincetown to Nauset Inlet. I slept on the beach in the dunes above the tide. They wouldn't allow you to do that anymore, I suppose. As I walked, I got a feeling for the expanse of the sea. The world felt suddenly spacious."

"We must reserve a back shop all our own, entirely free, in which to establish our real liberty and our principal retreat and solitude," wrote Montaigne. The studio was John Hay's back shop, the place where he conducted his private business. "It's like a fortress up there, with the winding road and the hill," a friend of John's had said to me before I visited. "He's got a buffer from all the busyness. I'm surprised he hasn't built a moat." The study was a bunker within the fortress, the most impenetrable spot in a generally impenetrable place.

In the corner of the studio I noticed a sort of compost heap of manuscripts and letters growing out of the closet. I later discovered that these were old journals and papers and drafts, some more than forty years old, lying there moldering and chewed by mice.

A less organic sight was the bulky sci-fi magnifying machine that sat on a desk in the middle of the studio. Without it, John could no longer read. Ironically, throughout his career John had written beautifully about acuity of vision, in both bird and man. The importance of *seeing well* was a perpetual theme. What's more, it could be said with no exaggeration that John Hay was a visionary. Many other nature writers pointed to him as kind of prophet, and I had noticed that quite a few of the articles I'd read about him also called him a "prophet of nature."

If this seemed a lofty title for an old guy on a hill, I had to admit that a large part of John's life work *had* been visionary. A prophet's job is to see and show, and just a quick dip into his books proved that John was in the business of opening eyes. How could people miss the sheer beauty of this world? The miraculousness right under their noses? And how could they fail to see that there were resources a thousand times more valuable than oil? All you had to do was get out into that world and look around. John felt compelled to warn people about the wonder of what was being lost, and had spent a lifetime doing so in the most emphatic possible language.

I wrote about nature, too, though with the irony and detachment endemic to my generation. I had grown up reading *Mad* and watching *Saturday Night Live,* and using the word *love* when it came to land always made me wince a little. But John seemed to feel the loss of species and land on a personal level, as if someone were cutting off his own limbs, and he tried to communicate that loss to others so as to avoid it. He knew that by destroying this wild world of so-called nature, we are destroying much more than we comprehend. We are destroying not just "species" and "habitats" but individual beings whose lives and consciousnesses, though different, are every bit as complex and interesting as our own.

Though John's writing always contained a personal vision, his books were also, in another way, almost entirely impersonal, if *personal* means cluttered by the details of an individual life. Though he wrote in the first person of his own wanderings in nature, he managed, to an almost uncanny degree, to get outside himself and into the lives of the birds, the fish, even the trees. In this way he was a forerunner, anticipating one of the major movements in environmental thought. This movement, to oversimplify, was from the anthropocentric, or human-centered, to the biocentric and ecocentic. Or, to put it even more bluntly, from a philosophy that puts man first to one that primarily considers the balance of the ecosytem and respects the validity of animal and vegetable life. John Hay's contribution, in part, was to stretch the boundaries of perception, calling anthropocentrism into question by exploring the possibilities of biocentric thought. Back in 1961, when people would look at you funny if you said the word *ecology* or *environment*, John began turning out books that vigorously argued the world was a community of sentient beings, all with their own varied and valuable consciousnesses, and that mankind's arrogance not only got in the way of our joining this rich community but led to our destruction of it.

Over the next forty years, employing a technique of passionate empathy, John threw himself outward, into the lives of birds and fish, articulating and anticipating a way of thinking about the world that was radical and vibrant. In his pages the persona known as "John Hay" often had an almost ethereal lightness, an ability to disappear or take on the color of his surroundings, like a caterpillar chewing on a leaf.

But now this visionary could barely see words on a page.

"How are your eyes?" I asked him when I'd finished with my other questions.

"Well, I got one cataract removed and that helps. The left one is still foggy. I'm going to have another operation on that later. It doesn't really help me read, though, it just makes things clearer. It makes your face clearer, it makes the leaves clearer, you know. But I still can't read print very well."

His face sank with the thought of being denied books, but then he stood and waved his cane, as if dismissing these worries. He announced that he needed to take a short break.

"Sometimes I think many of the world's problems could be solved if people just stepped outside and looked around," he said. Then he stepped outside himself to take a leak in the trees by the side of the studio, another ritual he had performed for fifty years or more. While he was outside I checked to see if the tape was picking up his voice, and listened to it for a minute.

When he came back, I was still fiddling with the little machine.

"I apologize for my rambling," he said, pointing to the recorder. "I'll cut down on the rambling."

"Please don't—this is great," I said. "And the acoustics in this room are great. The tape picks up everything."

"Ah-hah," he said. "So it's very *clear* rambling."

He laughed his infectious laugh, a series of rapid and joyous *heh*'s, and I laughed with him.

We talked for a little longer and then agreed to call it a day. He adjusted the thermostat and turned off the studio light by sharply yanking the cord that ran from the socket. We closed up the studio and walked down the path, our shoes crunching through the leaves. I wanted to reach out and hold his arm to steady him but knew it would be presumptuous, and possibly insulting. We paused by my car, and he told me one last story.

"The worst thing we've been doing over the past years is forgetting about localities. You forget about localities, individual places, and it's much harder to find out where you live. When I first moved here, I knew an old Cape Codder who said this place was getting filled up with people who didn't know where they were. And when you are displaced, you start to think everything is money. Money is the only purpose for so many people now, and they just accept this mindlessly. When I was studying with the poet Conrad Aiken, I met a descendent of Melville's named Paul Metcalf. Metcalf put together an anthology of great Indian writing, and he told a story about Roger Williams, the founder of Rhode Island. Williams was ousted by the Puritan colony in Massachusetts—they were pretty tough in the early days. He was kicked out of his house by the authorities and had to leave his wife and children in the middle of winter. He got as far as what would become the Rhode Island colony, and he was helped by the Wampanoag Indians along the way. The Wampanoags gave him food and drink and helped him get to where Providence is now, where he found a pure water spring. There the sachem, the local leader, said, 'We know you are interested in land. We will not sell land for English money. But you can have all you want for love.'"

John seemed finished, so I thanked him and shook his hand goodbye. But before I climbed into the car, he touched my shoulder and reemphasized the point of the story.

"It's hard for people to get the idea these days," he said softly, almost in a whisper. "They build these giant houses and think they *own* and *control* everything. But you can't have any real land unless you realize how much there is of human experience, of love, involved. People think this is a soft idea, but it isn't, it's nugget hard. People just don't understand that."

The story gave him new life, and he asked if I would like to take a short walk before I left. We hiked slowly back down the winding driveway and then cut through the woods. All around us the oak trees swayed and soughed, leaves blowing and scraping along the drive as if they had lives of their own. John said that he had missed trees when he moved here, but now the woods had caught up with him. Over the last half-century, what had been bare stumped hill had become a fully wooded forest.

For a while we stood there, listening to the wind in the trees. I tried to imagine the land as John had found it when he came back from the war. The few trees that hadn't been cut down had been lost to blight, salt winds, and poor soil, and I remembered that somewhere John had described them as "standing like stripped spars." Back then he was still a beginner when it came to the natural world—in some ways he had remained a beginner—and he'd told me that at first he mistook the mourning dove's hollow cooing for a calling owl. But slowly he stumbled forward, and gradually he began to get on more familiar terms with his avian neighbors. During his daily tramps in these woods he encountered ruffled grouse, towhees, whippoorwills, and ovenbirds, and over time he learned their names and language.

The birds were not the only singers he encountered. To the north of the driveway, not far from where we stood, the land fell off toward a depression known locally as Berry's Hole, where he would hear the tiny frogs called spring peepers sing every April, setting the whole place vibrating.

I thought about his description of how the place, despite the lack of trees, had grown on him. And I wondered when it had first occurred to him that this was where he would make his stand, and his name; that this was where he would make sense of things in the face of the world's chaos; and that this was where his sentences would come from. It took a lifetime to get to know the land, a slow and irregular process. But those first important steps of commitment must have been exciting.

Despite John's old-fashioned lifestyle, his was not homespun wisdom of the "quaint" variety. No, what John was up to on Dry Hill was something different. Here he began to sense that we all have our worthless woodlots, that we all have opportunities where we least expect them. Finding home would be the story of his life, a story he would tell again and again. But his notion of home, for all its traditionalism, was also radical. It is one thing to stay mindlessly in a place, out of inertia, but quite different to consciously bond with the land. It turned what was stagnant into a dramatic notion of lifetime commitment and digging down into place, and it was also a hard-earned notion. It had grown not just out of these woods on Dry Hill but out of taking a wild risk on this once stunted land.

It turned out that Franklin Ellis, the man who sold John the place, had mistakenly handed over eighteen acres, not ten. A few acres either way didn't matter much back then. But the value that human beings put on the same land had changed dramatically over the years. What had cost John $250 total would now sell for more than $250,000 an acre. Waving his cane, he had had to drive more than one covetous developer off his land. The space that had drawn John here was vanishing fast, as it was almost everywhere, and Dry Hill now stood like a wild island amid the Cape's ever-accelerating development.

We headed back up to the house, and when we got there he pointed up at the roof.

"As the trees grew, you could no longer see the ocean from our yard," he said. "So we built a small deck on the roof. Kristi and I would climb up there and eat our lunch with the water in sight. It was important not to lose touch with the water."

Then he told me something that I would turn over in my head for a long time. He admitted that he had had many doubts about his strange choice of coming to this place—"in the middle of nowhere"—and staying. "But then I would remind myself of a dream I had when I first returned," he said. In the dream, his newly built house was a ship, floating on the waters of Cape Cod Bay, bobbing up and down on the waves. No longer planted in the earth on Dry Hill, the house sailed like a schooner across the ocean.

Though much of what he said was enigmatic, I thought I understood this. In his case, staying still had been a journey, a voyage. And he had, much to his own surprise, discovered the world on Dry Hill.

2

A Good-Luck Gannet Day

I watched fall come in from our house on the edge of the sea. It was the kind of house we all dream of owning, not particularly large or impressive in its own right but situated perfectly, looking out over a shadowed green lawn at the ocean. The bed upstairs, something larger than a king—two queens pushed together, I think—also faced the water, so that you could spend an hour or so each afternoon pretending to read while watching the waves splash hard over this one crowned rock, white froth luminescent in the low light, water kicking up, then sliding down the rock's backside in white rivulets.

It sounds pastoral, and it was, but it was also cheap. We made rent by dog-sitting and paying as close as we could come to $500 a month, the catch being that we needed to be able to accept impermanence, knowing that we would be kicked out each summer, when the place rented for five times that per week. There was always a sense of tem-

porary encampment, of moving in or moving out, but that fit the overall mood. The house on the edge was not a place for certainty.

Upstairs, next to the bedroom, was an irregularly shaped room,
probably once a child's bedroom, which I had turned into a study.
It was like a ship's cabin, with my desk pointing toward the small
window, and it was through that window that I had first seen the gannets dive. In the days after my visit to Dry Hill, my desk became covered with a small mountain of books and articles by and about John
Hay. I spent the mornings reading about his life and the afternoons
searching Parnassus for more books. Parnassus was a used bookstore in
Yarmouth, with sagging floorboards and nooks and crannies and thousands of books piled up to the twenty-foot ceiling. Its proprietor was
the equally classic and appropriately named Ben Muse, who jotted
down book orders on scraps of paper that looked as though they would
never be seen again (but somehow he always got me my book). As October deepened, the mountain grew. I burrowed into John's life, deciding that I definitely had to write a biography of the man.

I also drove over to the *Cape Cod Times* to look for articles about
John. One of the articles I found was written by North Cairn, a nature
writer who looked to John as her mentor and model. The piece described how he came to the Cape after the war. "Everything was being
blown apart by human will and accident," he told Cairn. Cairn wrote:
"Hay perceived it as a rending—of consciousness and commitment—
and he would spend a lifetime trying, through his writing and other
work, to understand and describe how it might be restored to har-
mony." It was on Dry Hill that John began to heal that rending.

From my reading I learned that John had been born a child of privilege in 1915 and had grown up roaming the wilds of Manhattan. I also knew that the names of his ancestors were sprinkled not just through the society pages but through the history books. For instance, his grandfather, with whom he shared his name, was an elegant diplomat and popular poet who served as Lincoln's personal secretary during the Civil War and, forty years later, as secretary of state under Teddy Roosevelt. A refined, charming, and dapper little man—he stood five feet, two inches—John Milton Hay had been equally at ease negotiating for the Panama Canal and composing a sonnet. He, like his grandson, had a strong sense of propriety, and as his biographer wrote, "No matter how merry you were, no one slapped John Hay on the back." Near the end of his life, Hay's wit and elegance had served as subtle counterpoints to Roosevelt's brash boisterousness.

The diplomat's son, Clarence Hay, worked as a curator of archaeology at the American Museum of Natural History in New York. Throughout John's childhood, Clarence was often traveling with archaeological expeditions to the Yucatán, and John grew up fascinated by the Mayan artifacts his father brought home—and by the paintings of birds and the stuffed snowy owl in the hallways of the Hays' summer home at Lake Sunapee. The Sunapee land had been purchased by his famous grandfather, and it was in the woods around that New Hampshire lake that John first experienced the mystery of nature. He would later write that those days were his earliest glimpse behind the veil at another kind of life, a wild life different from the proper one he had learned in the city. At Sunapee he piloted the lake in a houseboat he built, with his pet goat and Airedale as first mates, and he camped along the shore and stared up at the stars and listened to Indian stories. At night he read James Fenimore Cooper and heard rumors of wolves, and in this time before television his love of books grew, rivaling his love of the woods. "We didn't have radio for a long time, and obviously we didn't have television," he said in the Cairn interview. "So I read a great deal. It was books, books, books."

John was shipped off to prep school as a young man, and later to Harvard. His love of books, especially of poetry, deepened, but he almost failed math. He was a dreamy adolescent, nicknamed "Foggy Hay" at school. It would come as a surprise to everyone in the Hay family when John eventually ended up writing about science.

As a writer I have always been ambitious—too ambitious, I think now. I must admit that from the start I saw John's Hay life as great "material." Something I could "use," I suppose.

The truth is that I tend to get a little overexcited about my projects, and John was becoming a project. So it was strange to come downstairs from an October morning embroiled in my books to find that my project had left a message on my answering machine. First of all, it was strange to hear John Hay's voice on the machine, like finding I had a message from Thoreau. And there was the fact that somehow I thought John wouldn't understand how to use the machine, having been born, as he was, before the end of World War I. But when

I came downstairs, there it was, as clear as day. "I was hoping you would like to get out and try to see some birds," he said.

I was happy and relieved, glad that my visit to his house had gone well enough, in his eyes, to prompt the phone call. I called back immediately, but he wasn't there, and if he knew how to use an answering machine, he wasn't quite modern enough to own one. I went to work for a while and then tried again; he picked up after the first ring.

"Would you be interested in a walk by the shore?" he asked hopefully. He sounded like an expectant child.

"That sounds wonderful. How about I pick you up in an hour?"

"Perfect."

An hour later I was driving up the leaf-strewn driveway to his house, the road now so covered and camouflaged by the season's detritus that on my first attempt I missed the turnoff. At the top of the hill John was waiting outside, with his binoculars around his neck and a bird book in hand. He climbed gingerly into my Honda Civic, and I got out to close the door for him. I had brought along a copy of one of his books that I'd bought at Parnassus, *Nature's Year*. I hoped he would sign it, but I didn't want to bother him with it right away. We decided that we would search for gannets, and John suggested we start in East Dennis, my neck of the woods. I asked if he had anyplace in mind.

"Anyplace there happens to be *boids*."

I decided to drive him over to the landing next to our house. On the way we passed the giant trophy home that was being built next door, its recently added cupola jutting like an ugly redundancy from the house's high roof. "Oh boy, thar she blows" John said. "It looks like a prison with a turret on top. That's the tower where the guard shoots the escapees from."

This was the same giant house that I had written about and that had prompted John's first call to me. One of the many appalling aspects of the house was how little satisfaction its owner seemed to get out of it. He was always either building a wall or tearing a wall down, planting this or uprooting that. On any given day the backward beeping of machines and the roar of tractors destroyed the peace that many of us had come to the neighborhood to find. If this man did get pleasure from his house, it seemed to be the pleasure of ordering around an army of workers.

"My God, look at that," John said. "A monument to waste. You were too kind to him in your essay. You should have gone for the throat."

He gestured toward the house and began to recite a poem from memory. His voice was low and sonorous.

"My name is Oxymandias, king of kings,
Look on my works, ye mighty, and despair!"
Nothing besides remains: round the decay
Of that colossal wreck, boundless and bare
The lone and level sands stretch far away.

"Shelley," he mumbled, and then he pointed at the house again. "That, right there, is the whole problem," he said firmly. "Unbridled vanity.

We make things larger and larger just as the world is asking us to make things smaller and more modest. We don't listen, so we don't hear what the world is saying to us."

He sighed, and I drove on. I circled around the cranberry bog and pulled in at the landing. From there we had a sweeping view of the bay, the eelgrass on the beach lighting the foreground with its orange fire. Staring down through our binoculars, we quickly proved ourselves to be nature writers, not naturalists, since we both had trouble telling whether the birds on the rocks were great cormorants or double-crested cormorants. We were both handicapped in this, me by performance anxiety and John by poor vision. But John was farsighted, if anything, and soon determined that they were greats and that the annual changing of the cormorant guard, from double-crested in summer to greats in winter, had recently occurred. In the course of this determination we fumbled with the bird book and laughed at our ineptitude.

Because of high tide the rocks were mostly covered and the usual bird congregation was absent. We were disappointed not to see gannets, and we decided to try another site. I suggested Paine's Creek, *his* neck of the woods, and he agreed.

"I'm on my own this week," I told him on the drive over.

He asked where my wife was, and I said she was at a retreat in western Massachusetts, working on her historical novel about Emily Dickinson.

"That's quite a hard thing to do. Especially since you don't have Emily around to talk to."

I agreed that it was difficult work trying to dig into and reimagine the poet's life.

"The Dickinsons are a hard family to figure out," he said. "There was a wall around them."

I explained that like me, my wife tended to get excited about her projects. "Nina has a bulletin board over her desk with pictures of the Dickinson homestead, maps of Amherst, the famous silhouette of Emily—everything about her."

John thought about this for a second. "It's like my gathering of feathers and skeletons when I was trying to imagine the lives of the terns."

I nodded. "Nina has read every book in the world about the Dickinsons, but pretty soon she's got to dive in and tell the story. I told her, 'You know enough. Don't overburden yourself with too much knowledge.'"

"Yes, knowledge only hints at things—underlying things. That's where psychology comes in. Intuition is key. It makes leaps that rational thought never can. But even with intuition, writing about Emily is going to be a challenge. I've met a lot of shy and retiring people in my life. They're hard to know."

I thought but didn't say that getting to know John Hay was also something of a challenge. Though he was alive and well and in my car, an advantage Nina didn't have, John was no slouch when it came to layers of defensiveness and complication. *Close but not too close.* As well as seeming as if he'd stepped out of an earlier century, he often gave one a sense of deep reserve. Just as his grandfather's biographer had said that no one would dare slap John Milton Hay on the back, I could no more imagine slapping *my* John Hay on the back than suggest we go skinny-dipping.

On the drive along the shore I stopped the car to point out a place on the beach where a new seawall was being constructed to combat erosion. The place was marked by little wooden surveyor's stakes with pink-orange plastic strips on top.

"Ah yes," John said. "The flags of doom."

We both knew that all the studies suggested that revetments and other seawalls were worthless over the long haul.

"But people don't listen," he said. "They prefer the illusion of control." He thought for a second before speaking again. "The sea has the last word. Maybe that should be the final sentence of my final book. Right before I die."

We drove away from the beach and out to Route 6A, then turned off and headed north, toward Paine's Creek. As we came down the small hill to the Paine's landing, a sharp-shinned hawk flew across the road and into the woods, flashing its beautiful ringed fan of a tail, and we gave each other "Did you see that?" looks. I parked facing the ocean, and right away we knew we had come to the right place. On the horizon, above the bay, a line of eiders flew from west to east. They looked like a long cursive sentence, occasionally humping into uppercase.

We climbed out of the car and made the short walk over the rocks to the beach.

"I drove Conrad Aiken down here when he was sick," John said.

I knew from my reading that the reason John had visited Cape Cod in the first place was to study with the famous poet Conrad Aiken. After college, John had lived in the Aikens' home and done yardwork in the morning and copied down sonnets in the afternoon.

"It was as if Conrad wanted to be on hallowed ground," he said.

I sat on a rock and John lay down in the warm sand, propping himself up on his elbow so he could look out at the water with his binoculars.

"We would drink orange juice and gin—he called them orange blossoms. When we came down from Boston, we would stop at the Howard Johnson parking lot for our first drink. And then we would pull in here for a drink to celebrate having arrived."

John lifted his binoculars to his eyes. There was activity every-where, and he was instantly absorbed. From where we sat we could watch several levels of bird life, from near to far. Closest to shore were the gulls, chattering and yakking, jockeying for position as the tide began to flow out of the creek. A few cormorants mixed in with the gulls out on a small island of grass, and beyond that a covey of Brant geese. Behind the Brants the line of eiders now stretched and humped all the way across the horizon from Sesuit toward Orleans. The place was alive: different birds flying in different directions in different styles.

John particularly delighted in the Brants. "It's something about the coloring of their heads that I love," he said. Sheer black, except for a few faint white slashes, covered the birds from the neck up.

While he focused on the geese, I studied a single bird that had landed close to us, on the end of the jetty. I glanced back and forth between it and my bird book, not quite able to tell whether it was an American golden plover or a black-bellied plover but enjoying the speckled black-and-white mosaic of its wings. As if for comic relief, a yellowlegs came stilting across the sand before flying wildly back up the creek.

After a while the wind came in, carrying a bit of the coming season, a hint of whitecaps frothing up over the bay.

"It's getting a little colder," I said. "Maybe the gannets will be firing up soon."

"You think they need cold? It's fish that they're after."

"But I associate them with cold. I call it gannet weather."

I make no pretensions to clairvoyance, but that day it was almost as if I called up the birds. Within five minutes I saw the first group massing out near where the old target ship used to sit. The target ship was a honeycombed wreck, once used for bombing practice by the military, that had now sunk completely. At first I mistook the birds for gulls, which is fairly easy to do from a distance. But then I walked right up to the shoreline and got a glimpse through the binoculars of the unmistakably long and radiant wings. I called for John to join me, and soon we were watching a full-on aerial show. The sun lit the undersides of the wings so that they blazed the same white as the breakers, and as we watched the birds hovered, tilted, and then dove into the water like white arrows.

I felt as if we were watching a thrilling sporting event as dozens more of the gannets gathered, clearly having found a great fishing spot. What was it like to be a fish and suddenly have a bird come hurtling down from above, out of the air into water, *your* element? If I felt for the fish, it didn't interfere with the sheer pleasure I took in the gannets' athleticism. One immature bird turned a full 360 degrees before striking the water, flashing from its dark back to its white belly. Once the gannets found a spot, they hit the water relentlessly. In a single second four, five, six birds would blade into the sea. Bird after bird dove, and splash after splash went up like the spouts from the blowholes of tiny whales. We cheered them on mindlessly.

"Boom!" I yelled when one hit the water. Then, "Boom! Boom! Boom!"

If not acting quite as foolishly as I, John was having fun, too. He wore a steady smile and laughed as the birds dove and rose back up, dove and rose again. This is what we had come to see.

"I'd like to be out there with them," he said.

"I thought birds were supposed to be energy conservers," I said.

"Not gannets," he said. "They're excessive."

We began to wonder how many fish a day gannets would need to survive, particularly given their wild expenditure of effort. He asked me how many fish an osprey caught a day, and I said three or four, though sometimes more once the clutch of nestlings hatched.

Suddenly John turned from the gannets and swept his right arm toward the horizon and then, pivoting, back behind him at the estuary. It was like standing inside a moving painting, the wind blowing the water and sand, the jangling light spraying over the beach, the colors and feel of the wind bracing us.

"I love the way the whole landscape is rhythmically alive," he said. That was how it seemed. I suggested the notion that it was like a painting, but he had other ideas.

"But there is so much movement. One movement leading to another. More like a symphony."

And he was right. The landscape was a kind of musical composition that the gannets were part of. The whole of it, the pulsing, the wildness, the rhythms, ran through us like a great electric current. We were part of something larger, and that thing that we were part of was vital. Was *alive*.

There were moments that I felt there was a impenetrable bubble around John, but there were other moments when the bubble was gone and he was very much *there*. During my research I'd stumbled upon an essay about Thoreau and John Hay by the writer Frederick Turner. The essay concluded with Turner and Hay hiking up Mount Katahdin. Turner was in his early forties at the time, but he found that his almost seventy-year-old companion had little problem keeping pace on the arduous climb.

In the essay, Turner asked John if he ever still felt like a kid. " 'Sure,' Hay answered. 'All the time. Especially in my dreams. I'll be seventy at the end of August. How does it happen that suddenly I wake up and find that I'm seventy?!' He looked at me with a fierce astonishment. 'But,' he went on, in a quieter tone, 'I hope I don't live to be so old I lose interest in the natural world. That would be death to me.' "

It was that look—of "fierce astonishment"—that still frequently broke through John's more proper veneer. And it was that look—his eyebrows lifted in their permanent arc and his blue eyes alive and his lips slightly raised in an openmouthed smile—that he wore as he watched the gannets. Delighted and fierce and proper all at once.

I felt close to him as we stood there watching the gannets, and I found myself telling him something I hadn't expected to. I admitted that lately I had been spending much of the time during my beach walks worrying and planning for the future. For the last few years Nina and I had tried to support ourselves as writers. But we knew that we couldn't afford to stay on Cape Cod much longer and that our pastoral adventure would soon end. We hoped to start a family, and we were always short on money. I had dreamed of writing a book that would solve these problems, but this had begun to seem increasingly unrealistic. It was getting harder to keep worry from working on my mind, and I was now using my walks to the bluff for therapy or planning sessions.

"You need to watch that," he said with surprising sharpness. "You're not really seeing nature at all if you're just listening to your own chatter. You can't come to it for your own uses. You've got to see it for itself. To open yourself to it. It isn't easy."

"For me, planning can be as bad as worrying," I said.

"We all need the illusion of control. Just like the seawalls and trophy homes. We need to preserve the myth that we're in charge. We don't like to face the fact that we're as vulnerable as skunks or shore-birds. But nature teaches that uncertainty and chance are enormous factors in the lives of animals, and it just so happens that we are ani-mals. If we admit that, it may not solve anything, but at least it has the advantage of being honest. And if we admit how truly vulnerable we are, then humility isn't just the wise choice, it's the obvious one."

When I wrote about nature, I often used it as a stage for human drama. But John was always pointing beyond the human. For him, emotion wasn't to be wasted on oneself but, through empathy, im-parted to other creatures and plants. To put it another way, the beach and the woods were places not for tunneling inward as much as going outward.

In his 1964 address accepting the John Burroughs Medal, na-ture writing's Pulitzer, John had said, "To see, and then to interpret, takes practice, and practice in depth." Reading his books over the past weeks, I had kept coming back to the importance of seeing well as his perpetual theme.

In fact, the more I read of his work and the more I talked to him, the more I understood that seeing meant everything to John Hay, and that was what excited me. Both the ability to see the miraculous na-ture of the world and the ability to see the consequences of one's life and actions. *To see!* That, after all, was the great discipline which na-ture taught. To make the effort—and it was an effort—to see without a cluttered, controlling mind. To see and respect other beings for what they were. To turn one's vision not inward, always inward, but out-ward, toward the multifarious world.

When we had arrived, we'd had the beach and the gannets to our-selves, but not long after a gray-haired couple showed up. They set up camp down the shore from us, where they watched the gannets through a telescope. After a while we walked over and asked if we could have a peek. As bird-watchers they were relative beginners, and they asked us what the birds were called. John began to expound on the gannets' habits, telling them of his visits to the gannetries on Bonaventure Island on the Gaspe Peninsula of Quebec.

The couple seemed very pleased. When he was finished, the woman addressed him almost bashfully. "Are you John Hay?" she asked.

John admitted he was. It was a funny moment: the oxymoron of the noncelebrity celebrity. Clearly this had been more than the cou-ple had bargained for when they took their brand-new telescope to the beach. They were getting their money's worth, seeing both spectacu-lar diving gannets and the Cape's famous celebrator of birds.

Through the scope the scene was even more immediate and vivid, and I felt almost as if I were part of the dive, becoming the great white birds as they searched the water, feeling the tension of hovering, then the release in a great wild plunge. Another line of eiders came hump-ing through, bisecting the view through the scope from west to east. And then a line of Brants, which were more haphazardly aligned. When John looked into the scope again, he muttered, "Yes... Wow, marvelous." Now we had eiders, scoters, plovers, Brants, killdeers, gulls, and cormorants covering the horizon, all trying to upstage each other, flying in every direction. A great whirl of birds.

"In the old days there were really a lot of birds around," he said. "But this isn't half bad."

To me it seemed a little more than that. If exaltation took practice, as John had written, then I'd practiced plenty since moving to Cape Cod. But the moments of delight had almost always come while I was walking alone. There was something about being both with John and with the birds that lifted this day above the ordinary.

"It's quite a wonderful time of year, isn't it?" he said. "It's a changeover. All the migrants come and go, and the winds go with them. A time for movement and transition."

We went back to watching the gannets, but soon the north wind picked up and a more seasonable cold blew in. We decided to retreat to the car. Before we did, the speckle-backed plover flew near again, and watching it and its reflection in the shallow water, I told John that I was now sure it was a black-bellied. He confirmed my identification.

"That was marvelous," he said as we walked back to the car, "Just marvelous. I'm afraid I'll have to be getting back home. I'm exhausted now. But that was worth everything."

We climbed into the car and drove away from the beach. On Route 6A we passed the Cape Cod Museum of Natural History, which John had helped found and had become the first president of forty years before. Though he was temperamentally apolitical, his love for nature had transformed him into a leader, an activist, and he was still active in the museum's affairs. For decades he had served as its chief administrator, fundraiser and, of course, visionary. As we passed, he gestured at the museum and told me that he was anticipating a visit from its current director later that day. John didn't like the direction the museum had been heading in, and was particularly affronted by the fact that this new director didn't even live on the Cape but commuted here for work. And he was upset with the man over the firing of a young poet who had worked at the museum. John described to me how he'd like to drive the director off his property and "bawl him out."

"Maybe I should go in and buy a bottle of Jack Daniel's to prepare myself," he said when we passed the liquor store.

"You can slug back a few shots before he arrives."

"Well, yes. I better think about how to *behave* this afternoon. I don't want to just fly off the handle." He smiled.

We drove back up Stony Brook Road and pulled over to check his mailbox at the bottom of Dry Hill. The mail wasn't in yet, but we picked up the newspaper.

"It'll be the same news as yesterday," he said. "The world going to hell. It's terrifying."

But the experience on the beach had lifted him too high to let the paper drag him down. The open air had worked its alchemy, transubstantiating curmudgeonliness into wonder.

"I have an idea—" I said.

"What's that?" he interrupted. His voice was loud and playful. "You're going to turn yourself into a gannet, right? Then you can have some real fun." He laughed in his usual startled manner, and I forgot what I was going to say.

"Transformation," he said as he climbed out of the car. "That's the secret, transformation."

I walked him to the house, and we stood on his front porch for a while, talking.

"There are larger rhythms than just our human rhythms," he said. "It's when we think our rhythms are the only noise, that's when we get in trouble. How do we stop jabbering long enough to hear something beyond ourselves? Living by the ocean helps, of course. It's harder to think you're so all-important when you have something so primal next door." He sighed and leaned against the door frame. "A day out with the birds," he said. "That's about as close as I can come to an answer."

He slipped into the house and came back with an old book. It was *Bird Display and Behavior*, by Edward A. Armstrong. He handed me the book and suggested I read the first chapter, "The Ceremonial of the Gannet."

"He writes about the importance of ritual in the gannet's life," he said. "Ritual is the key. The rituals of nest-building, courtship, and diving."

I thanked him for the book and we said goodbye. I drove off, but when I got to the bottom of the hill I noticed that the flag on his mailbox was now up. Driving back up the driveway with his mail, I no longer felt awkward or intimidated, as I had just a few weeks before; in fact, I felt an almost goofy comfortableness.

When I knocked again, he popped his head out. He thanked me for the mail. Then he mentioned the new museum director again.

"Give him a kick in the shin for me," I said.

"I'll give him a kick in the ass," he growled.

This time when I climbed back into the car I remembered that I'd brought along my copy of *Nature's Year*. I ran back to the house one more time and asked him to sign it.

"You won't go away," he said. But he walked out on the porch, took the book from me, pinned it against the house, and scribbled something in an unsteady hand.

"That was a marvelous outing," he said again, handing me the book. "Thank you for it."

This time I finally did leave, driving out through the arch of trees. I had come to John because I thought he would be good material, but I was quickly sensing that I might be getting more than I'd bargained for. Earlier in the day I had read a line in *Nature's Year*: "I regret the shorter day and the need to leave the great air so soon." I was already sorry that our adventure was over. Winter was blowing in, and the change from daylight savings had just occurred. I wondered if I would have much of a chance to get John outside during the coming cold months. "Old age is no good," he'd said earlier with a sigh. But at least we had had moments, and moments, it seemed to me, were what he had built his life on.

At the bottom of Dry Hill I pulled over and looked at his inscription on the title page of my book. It read:

To Dave,
On good-luck gannet day. October 31.
John

3

THE USE OF ELDERS

In November, Cape Cod transforms. The gannets continue to dive into the surf, and the cold shadows of gulls ripple over beach rocks. But the water, so inviting only weeks before, takes on a darker, bracing shade of blue, and the clouds bulk up purple and muscular. As the northeast winds bluster across the bay, it isn't hard to see why Cape inhabitants, from the native Wampanoags to the captains of clipper ships, have always chosen, quite sensibly, to winter away from the ocean.

Our own choice that coming winter was a less practical one. It was getting hard to open the front door into the wind, and one day when I walked outside a hundred starlings broke from the trees with an explosive sound like applause or hard rain on a shed roof. Often when I walked toward the beach I had to laugh at how overdone—*overblown*—it all was, real wind blasting as the real weather finally kicked in, bouncing the phone lines up and down and blowing the world from east to west, and suddenly fall was on its way out and winter roaring in. The wind sprayed another dozen birds overhead —finches with breasts stained reddish purple—and the sand rose in swarms and stung my arms, and the ocean roiled with whitecaps.

For sixty years John Hay had greeted the coming of winter outdoors, on his own terms. When I called in early November, however, he said he was not feeling well and was not up for any long walks. But he asked me to drop by and chat anytime I liked. I took him up on his offer a few days later.

Driving up onto Dry Hill with the trees stripped of their leaves felt like driving into another century. In the coming weeks, being around John would stretch my life back into the past of the place. During our meetings I always had a palpable sense that that past was nearby. And more and more those meetings were haunted by a ghost.

That ghost's name was Conrad. After graduating from Harvard, John had met the Pulitzer Prize–winning poet Conrad Aiken, a meeting that changed the course of his life. While the space on Cape Cod might have enticed him and the sea might have kept him here, it was Aiken who drew him to the Cape in the first place.

During one of our November meetings I asked John how he came to know Aiken.

"I sought him out, really," he said. "He and his wife, Mary, had a lovely house in England, down a cobblestone street in Rye, where Henry James and Joseph Conrad had lived. I visited them after I graduated from Harvard in '38 because a friend of mine had been in class with him at their little private summer school, where Mary taught art and Conrad taught writing. I stayed with them for a few days, marveling at the whole scene. I had this sense that Conrad and his wife might supply me with something I didn't have."

John explained that before he was drafted, he visited Aiken again at his house on Cape Cod. The house, poetically named 41 Doors, still sat right up the street from John's on Stony Brook Road. At the time, John told me, he had vague literary ambitions and was dreaming of being a poet while trying to work as a reporter. He stayed with the Aikens for a while, doing both yard and literary work, hoping to absorb whatever it was that made Aiken a writer. He talked to Aiken to "see if I couldn't get in a little apprentice writing with him when the war ended.

"It was Conrad's personality as much as his work that seemed almost immediately liberating, even thrilling, to me. My parents—my mother in particular—believed in being proper and restrained, and that was how I was raised. Conrad was entirely different. Wild and uninhibited. Daring. I was drawn to him."

War interrupted John's time with Aiken, but before he shipped out, he made an uncharacteristically impulsive decision, one that would affect the course of the rest of his life. A neighbor of Aiken's was offering to sell a plot of land on Dry Hill, and John, after some hesitation, decided to buy it. The land waited for him during the war.

Later in November, perhaps inspired by a stretch of warm and cloudless days, John and I decided to attempt a fairly ambitious walk: all the way from Dry Hill to the beach. In his younger days this had been his daily lap—down the hill through the oak woods, across the pasturelands to the dunes and beach, and back again—but he hadn't done it in over a year. But John was feeling strong again. He was walking without a cane, which pleased him, despite the fact that he enjoyed using the cane to point at and swat things.

Since his eyesight had started to fade, John had stopped driving (unlike a lot of his fellow Cape Cod retirees, who didn't give up their licenses just because they couldn't see). It was now his habit to walk everywhere around Brewster, and it was also his habit to disregard automobiles almost entirely. He strolled with a casual contempt for the cars, which foolishly assumed that they had the right of way, and it was a common sight in town to see him shuffling down the street. Not in the middle of the street exactly, but not on the side either.

A mutual friend had told me that one day he had been driving back to Brewster shortly after his move off-Cape. "I was driving down on 6A," he said, "and there was this old guy in rumpled, raggedy clothes walking along the highway, and I thought, 'Geez, Brewster really does have homeless people now,' and of course it turned out to be John."

Now, at the end of Stony Brook Road, I got to experience the adventure of crossing Route 6A with John. I watched as he waited for a pause in the traffic before darting across in a shuffling sprint. I'd noticed before that he crossed streets the way rabbits or squirrels do, pausing, listening, and then charging. Once, the very first time we met, I was standing with him on one side of 6A, waiting to cross to the Museum of Natural History, when he suddenly grew impatient and dashed blindly ahead. For a brief second I thought I was witnessing the death of America's greatest living nature writer: an oil truck barreled toward him and sounded its horn, while John waved his arms and his cane over his head, cursed, and shuffled across.

The crossing this time was without incident, however, and soon we were walking onto Quivett Neck. Though the native people are mostly gone, the native names remain. We stopped at the Quivett cemetery, where my father is buried. Among the stones were markers with another layer of names, those of old New Englanders like Thankful Homer and Barnabash Sears, as well as a headstone for Asa Shiverick, 1816–1894, the founder of the Shiverick Shipyard. I knelt and read out loud for John from a stone shared by a husband and wife:

Mrs. Mercy Crowell, died June 9, 1855, at 78.
Her husband, Captain William Crowell, was lost at sea, Sept. 2, 1806, age 31.
Their graves are sever'd far and wide
by mount & stream & sea.

"A long time to be a widow," John said.
After the cemetery we cut into the woods, walking on a sandy,

rutted road below a canopy of second-growth oaks and maples. This was the part of town known as Crowes Pasture. As we walked, the talk turned, as it often did, to Conrad Aiken.

"Conrad was a very brave man," John said. "I only really began to understand that after he died, after I got older myself and understood the daily fight he fought. He drove Kristi crazy, and he could be terribly offensive. But the thing was that his was the opposite of small talk. He *elevated* those around him. You might be sitting in the kitchen talking about dinner plans and he would barge in with his damn cat on his shoulders. Before you knew it, you were talking about life and death and ultimate concerns. It seemed to me he was having a constant dialogue with himself about no less than the supreme nature of being. It was exhilarating, really. You really couldn't spend much time worrying about everyday things when Conrad was around. He wanted to transcend the temporary.

"And his wife, Mary, was wonderful. She put up with him in a marvelous and courageous way. Conrad wasn't the most faithful husband, though. He liked to lay his hands on girls if they were pretty enough. There was one named Velva something-or-other, who snuck down to the Cape while poor Mary was in England. This girl had two young children, and one day they found Conrad's false teeth and flushed them down the toilet. My father wrote a little impromptu poem about it."

John stopped and thought for a minute, trying to recover the poem from memory. Then he smiled and recited it:

Children seeking new adventures,
Did a job on Conrad's dentures
Said Conrad, mumbling through his gums,
"With Velva one must take what comes."

When we reached the beach, we stopped and stared out at the ocean. John told me that he and Conrad had sometimes brought drinks down to the beach and watched the sea "like watching a good play."

"Conrad was so intent on exploring himself," I said. "But you chose to leave yourself behind."

John bristled a little. "Oh, I was pretty involved with myself, too," he said. "I was reading Jung and deciding between him and Freud. It was really a question of learning about myself and nature simultaneously. On the one hand it was a process of moving away from myself, moving toward uncertainty and mystery. But on the other it was getting to know myself. If I hadn't had that interest in psychology, then I wouldn't have gone as deeply into nature as I did."

"So going outside yourself was part of going in?"

"Well, it's not that simple, of course. It's not just walking into the woods and saying, 'Oh, here I am. I've found myself—isn't that nice?' It's rigorous work, leaving your own thoughts behind and focusing on following the footprints of a shrew or the diggings of a skunk. Certain preconceptions have to be left behind as well. It's a discipline, you see. The easiest thing is to let your thoughts boomerang back to yourself.

But you need to keep the mind and eyes turned outward. That's when the transformation starts. But really it *is* that simple. The way to start is to get out there.

"And yes, sure, looking outward and looking inward are intertwined. As John Muir said of a walk he took, 'By going outward I found I was going in.' There is always an underground relationship between us and the world we live in. That's why those who ignore so-called nature—who make fun of it, as if it were some dowdy, old-fashioned preoccupation—do so at their own risk. They forget that we all began in nature and that our words and culture were formed out of our relation to the animal world. We concern ourselves with names and facts and figures, and of course money, money, money, but all the while we sometimes forget that our lives are a secret conversation with the green world. We are still animals and we still react to weather, fire, and our animal kin. But I don't think you can understand nature at all without looking into yourself. The native people knew that. Theirs was not introspection so much as a different sort of looking. And of course if you begin to spend more time in the natural world, you feel yourself starting to change. You find you are recreated.

"I realized that nature is essential to everyone. Many people forget this, but it doesn't mean it's any less true. People who ignore nature feel something nagging at them, something missing, like a lost limb, and they never understand that they need to get outside into the world. They think they can work out problems of salvation within themselves, but that is a hopeless quest. What we all need is something more than ourselves. And that is where nature comes in. The outside world affects the inside world. The great tragedy of the twentieth century is that we have denied nature and imagined ourselves above it." He made a little dismissive wave toward the sand. "We've said, 'We're the big guys on the planet now. We're beyond nature. That stuff's not important to us.' Humility is the missing ingredient, of course. People think of humility as some passive thing, but it's hard work. Being humble enough to leave yourself behind and enter into places. To leap out of yourself. And then to gradually start to care."

He turned away from me, toward the water. "What is it that we're missing? I think we have an essential wildness in us that is too often stifled. That wildness builds up in us and becomes dark because we ignore it. When we go into nature, we are looking for a release, a dialogue." He paused as if finished but then continued. "We are searching for a match for that wildness inside us in the wild land." He gestured north, toward Provincetown. "And in the wild sea, of course."

On the way back home we decided to stop by 41 Doors. The house was still standing, in good shape, owned now by the Killoran family, though Joseph Killoran lived in the South. Killoran had been the editor of Aiken's letters and had befriended Mary Aiken in her later years while he was working on Aiken's biography. As I understood it, Mary Aiken had simply *given* Killoran the house.

Stony Brook Road had been cut and filled so that it now curved away from the front door of Aiken's house, but the old road was still there, serving as a sort of driveway for 41 Doors. That road was only about ten feet wide, pockmarked and rutted, with greenbrier and brambles encroaching on both sides. The house was a quirky Cape, the back of which stared out over an abandoned cranberry bog. It jutted with els and additions, just as Aiken had described it back in 1941: "There are more terraces to this house than there are in a Henry James novel."

John smiled at the house. "That place spilled over with a wildness its walls couldn't contain," he said. He shook his head. "People were much freer in those days. In their conversation. In their insults of each other. Every way. They weren't so sensitive about everything. So tightened up, the way people are these days."

I asked John if Aiken had helped loosen him up.

"Well, of course. You see, he was a poet, and the way he acted was like a poet. I had never encountered a creature like him. You know, my family was very proper, very New England, and they were always scared of such things. They thought you shouldn't express yourself too loudly and you shouldn't mention anything to do with your emotions, because somehow the roof would fall in. "Conrad wasn't like that. Deep down he was very shy, and so he acted truculent and obnoxious at times because he was shy. But he was very generous to young writers like me. He was also friends with the writer Malcolm Lowry, and they got drunk as skunks together. It was all a very dizzying experience.

"It was dizzying being with Conrad anyway. First of all, he had a constant obsession with the idea of consciousness. I never quite understood what he meant by it to begin with, but he was always probing into this greater consciousness. Even when he got drunk at night." John laughed out loud. "At the end of one drunken night I said, 'I suppose what you're trying to do is forget everything and join the eternal dream.' And Conrad said, 'That's quite right.'"

He paused and looked straight at me. His expression turned deadly serious. "Conrad had lots to forget, you see. His father suspected his wife of cheating. He shot her in their house in Savannah and then killed himself. Conrad was nine years old and had to go to the police station to report it. And you could see this all along in him—the attempt to get over it. He was forever conscious of having witnessed that moment—having seen his father and mother both killed. It makes for a tough life."

We sat there, both trying to imagine the unimaginable moment. After a few minutes I asked the only question that occurred to me.

"What did he look like?" I asked.

John immediately hunched up his shoulders to give himself bulk. "Oh, he was bull-necked, red-headed, with blue eyes. Dark blue eyes, like amethyst. He was of medium height but heavy. You could always hear his educated tone of voice. Pursing his lips at each word so you would understand." He imitated the lip-pursing. "He's the type that's gone out. You don't find many literary folks like that anymore. At least I haven't. Everybody seems to have dispersed."

We turned away from 41 Doors and began the walk back home.

"Conrad, you see, was *addicted* to conversation," he said. "He wanted to engage people. He figured conversation was his salvation, in a way. His parents' death hung over him like a dark weight his whole life. In response, he thought it vital to live right, and to live right you had to live the proper ritual. You had to drink the right drinks, and you were forbidden to drink anything else. For instance, he had these goblets down at his house, these pewter goblets with grape leaves on the side, a tribute to the ancient Greeks. And that's what you had to drink out of! A chalice! That staved off the evil eye. For a young guy like me, it was all very impressive."

"I've got to admit I'm jealous," I said.

"Why?" he said. "You don't have that kind of literary community over in Dennis these days? Hah! Nobody shows up over there but the damn gulls!"

He was laughing hard at this—at me, perhaps; I wasn't sure. I thought that if there was one thing I wouldn't have expected, having until the past year known John Hay only through his writing, it was how much he laughed. Before I'd begun my visits, I'd imagined that much of his conversation would be terribly earnest. But I had imagined wrong.

"I had this sense that he and his wife might supply me with something I didn't have," John had said. One thing the Aikens supplied him with was liquor. Back then, no living writer—not Bernard De Voto, with his evocation of the perfect martini, or the liquor-soaked Hemingway, or even Malcolm Lowry—could match Conrad Aiken when it came to the daily glorification of booze. "The ritual of cocktail hour represents the communion of all friendly minds separated in time and space," he wrote. His poetic elevation of cocktail hour grew so famous that even the napkins used with the Aikens' pewter goblets later found their way into an Updike novel. It was all very ritualized and elevated, and for the young John Hay the talk must have been only slightly less intoxicating: long, drunken monologues about poetry, art, consciousness, and dreams.

"My God, there was a lot of drinking going on in that house," John told the *Boston Globe* in 1995. "The gin, the parties, famous writers dropping in. I never wanted to leave."

If one of the roles of a mentor is to provide a different sort of parent, an alternate family, then Aiken fit the bill. "He helped me because he took me out of my traditional background," John said. "Which was so reserved."

A photograph from the late 1940s captures some of that time's magic. The Aikens and the Hays stand close together in front of a statue in the backyard of 41 Doors. They hold the always-present drinks in front of them. Conrad appears slightly rumpled and perturbed, like someone's angry dad, while Mary, his much younger wife, smiles with obvious spirit—"She was the one who held it all together," John told me. The young Hays look like movie stars. Kristi in shoulder pads evokes Lauren Bacall, while John—young, dark, and handsome—stares, square-jawed, at the camera.

Of course, below the sheen of smiles and cocktails lay a deep uncertainty. "I still had no great confidence in my abilities," John would write. He had his doubts about both himself and his vocation. It was not then a foregone conclusion that he would shape sentences and books out of the Cape's wilderness. In fact, at the moment the camera clicked he was more than a decade away from stumbling onto his true subject. And the picture couldn't possibly show how Kristi felt about being dragged out to the edge of the earth to start her adult life. Did it seem like a conscious exile? A banishment?

Of all the roles a mentor serves, perhaps the most obvious, and most important, is to show that *it can be done*, that it—in this case, an artistic life—is possible. Although John hadn't yet written a single book and indeed was many years from completing his first important work, he could at least glimpse in Aiken how this sort of life might be lived. As for Aiken, what did he gain by taking in this young man who had approached him out of the blue? It may seem strange that he invited John Hay, whom he barely knew, to come and live at his home before the war. But if young men naturally seek out alternate fathers, then maybe older men look to surrogate sons for support, energy, and, of course, friendship.

In late November I drove over to the Cape Cod Museum of Art. There I paid the fee and walked inside to look for the sculpture that I knew I'd find. In the far room I saw a bronze bust on a wood block. Even before I checked the name I knew the head. Conrad Aiken's bulldog countenance, in full Churchillian glower, stared back at me. He was as John had described: an imposing figure with a big head, heavy cheeks, and a large aquiline nose. The plaque below the sculpture confirmed that it was Aiken and said that the sculptor was Arnold Geissbuhler. I stared Aiken down for a while, trying to imagine being in his presence. By the time I left I could picture him better: barely able to rise from his stuffed chair because of his bulk, pontificating through pursed lips, enunciating every word, and, as Joseph Killoran had written of him, "speaking in full paragraphs."

"He spoke in a clipped, educated way," John had said, echoing how I felt about the way he himself spoke. "You wouldn't believe it if you heard it today."

I drove away from the museum, not exactly feeling that I had been in Aiken's presence but having a slightly better sense of what it would have been like.

After my visit to the museum, I drove to the Brewster Ladies' Library to dig into a box that held notes and photographs left over from an old exhibit on Aiken. I also found a copy of a speech that John had made to kick off an Aiken tribute. The head librarian told me that the talk had been given behind the library, not in it, and unfortunately it had been a windy day. John didn't quite have the hang of the microphone, and his words blew east toward Orleans, so that only those in the front row could hear them. But John being John, the rest of the audience sat patiently and nodded in appreciation. Though he had come a long way and achieved much in the course of a lifetime, it was a classic performance by Foggy Hay, sending his poetic words off into the wind.

I thanked the librarian and made a copy of the speech. On the way home I decided to run by and take John's mail up the driveway for him. He thanked me, and I showed him one of the photos I'd found of Aiken, portly and stiff, jammed into his thronelike chair. "Good lord, he looks like he's on the electric chair," John said.

Before I left, he asked me how my "historical studies" were going, and I told him I had been reading up on Conrad Aiken.

"The Cape has always been a place for separatists," he said. "For pilgrims. Are you a pilgrim? Conrad certainly was. Do you know what it says on the bench beside his gravestone?"

I said I didn't.

"'Cosmic Mariner: Destination Unknown,'" he said with a laugh, shaking his head. "A little silly maybe, but no joke. He was always searching. Sometimes I think what he found in consciousness was what I found in nature. Sometimes I think the two places are not so different. It was the mystery that interested him. Being open to the mystery. A place beyond words."

When I got home I retreated to my study and my mountains of books and papers and chewed over the gifts that Conrad Aiken had given John Hay. It still required an act of the imagination for me to picture John not as the gray eminence he now was but as a relatively insecure and uncertain young man. "There is a wonderful kind of old-fashioned restraint in John Hay's books," wrote the environmental scholar John Elder. But what I now saw as reserve was then shyness, though I couldn't ignore the fact that John had had the nerve to approach a famous older writer in the first place. Aiken, of course, had helped make John. It was conceivable that John would have become who he was without contact with Aiken, but it was also entirely possible that he wouldn't have. Aiken had offered John Hay what the Cape writer Bob Finch once told me that John had offered him: "a sense of what was possible."

It seemed to me that Aiken had also offered John no less than a new and daring way to be in the world. All through his childhood John Hay had felt pulled by two different forces, the restraint and propriety of his "seldom exuberant" parents and the wildness and freedom that he first felt when exploring the woods around Lake Sunapee. He had glimpsed a hidden wildness on the lake in his houseboat, at his secret campsites on the shore, in the stuffed owl in the hallway, in the trinkets brought home by his father from the Yucatán, in the Indian stories he heard at night, and later in Walt Whitman's poetry, which sounded "like a fresh voice out of incomparable space." Unlike the voice of his parents, this secret voice rang with exuberance. But to devote his life to searching for this unnamable wild contact ran counter to everything his parents had tried to teach him. His parents—again, especially his mother—had prized the Yankee virtues of self-reliance, austerity, and reserve, and judging himself by those standards, John felt like a failure. "The self-made man was very much admired," he wrote. "I did my best to follow such examples, but I was always falling short."

What Aiken had given John, then, among other things, was a new way to judge himself. "The life that men praise and call successful is but one kind," wrote Thoreau. "So I began to learn about detail and what it might lead to," John wrote of his teenage years, "like a bobolink nesting in the meadow, the color of a grackle's eyes, the beak of swallows or of hawks. Someone was starting to lift the corner of the curtain for me." It would take a while, but John Hay would gradually become a forceful voice in a kind of Thoreauvian countertradition, and he would lead a life that valued things other than the traditional definitions of success and sobriety and money. In other words, he would learn to follow what had instinctively interested him as a child—the wildness and the mystery, things that his parents, and his schooling, had tried to squelch in him. It was Aiken who helped give him the courage to follow this less-traveled path.

But it wasn't that simple. The best teachers don't tell you how to be; rather, they reveal to you who you are. What we sometimes forget is that they often reveal this by the ways in which they are unlike us. For years John mulled over Aiken's notion of consciousness, but he finally took it in a direction that had never occurred to Aiken. One day, while watching the freshwater herring leap upstream during their spring migration, John began to understand that this notion of consciousness extended not just to human beings but to all creatures. "Do we belabor the special nature of consciousness too much, as if it were some kind of A-1 badge that separated mankind from the rest of animate creation?" he wrote in *The Great Beach*. "Consciousness must be infinitely more mysterious, more connective, than any attributes we may assign it of personal distinction." It isn't that man isn't unique, he discovered, but that all creatures are.

This revelation also led to his first true intellectual split with Aiken. In the book *Spirit of Place*, the environmental writer Frederick Turner describes a hike on Mount Katahdin with John Hay and quotes John's recollection of that break:

> One day during this period, I was out along a stream there in Brewster and saw the herring coming upstream against the current, and it suddenly came to me: this is the Life Force. I'd been missing the connections between all natural phenomena that are tied together by this thing. It had tremendous impact on me.
>
> Later, having a drink with Conrad in the backyard of his house, I observed that consciousness, about which he had so much to say, was a shared thing, that humans weren't the only thing in the universe that were conscious. "Nonsense!" he said. "Sheer nonsense! You're barking up the wrong tree there. You've bought the Schweitzer stuff about reverence for all life. *We are superior!*"
>
> Well, we weren't at all. That's what's so wonderful about a place like Katahdin: it shows us our limits. If we really look at nature, we see this every day. But we don't know how to look. If we did, we'd see those limits, and we'd see how much life there is that hasn't anything to do with us but is absolutely right just where it is.

And with that it was time to start leaving Conrad and his obsessive internal explorations behind. John would not go down Conrad's path. The fish had helped him find his own theme, his own way.

The idea of going to an older writer to become an apprentice now seems hopelessly outdated. But it worked for John, though perhaps in ways he hadn't expected. At their best, these mentor-apprentice relationships are complex beyond mapping, going far beyond the obvious cliché of kneeling at the feet of the wise man or even learning by example. When the relationship is truly working, it always contains an element of necessary rebellion. Keats, for instance, learned twice from his early mentor, Leigh Hunt, first assimilating the older poet's style and then turning away from its excesses. And for John Hay, who leaned on Conrad Aiken during his break from his parents' proper world, the subtle break from Aiken himself was just as important. Lawrence Buell, a recent biographer of Emerson, writes that Emerson was an "anti-mentor," eventually creating the giants that killed him. All the best mentors, it seems to me, are also anti-mentors. They help us to our feet, but once there, we walk alone. They give us someone to define ourselves not just by but against.

4

Digging In

In December I dropped by Dry Hill unannounced. A foot of snow had fallen, and I wondered how the Hays were making out. But John wasn't home, and I was about to turn around and drive away when I saw Kristi dragging a Christmas tree through the snow in the side yard. I knew that she had hurt her back during a fall and she was using crutches that wrapped around her forearms to help her walk. Still, she pulled the tree with one arm and with the other stabbed through the snow with a single brace. I ran from the car and grabbed the tree and carried it into the house.

I hadn't spent much time alone with Kristi. Now, once the tree was safely inside the house, we had a chance to chat for a minute on the porch. If Kristi Hay was no longer the Lauren Bacall beauty of the early pictures, she still had a remarkably open and appealing face, now framed by short white hair. Since I knew that she had studied taxidermy, I told her about the great horned owl I had recently found on the beach. Even in death there was something strong and fierce about the bird; its black talons were still sharp enough to cut my fingertip when I picked it up, and its black-striped feathers shone a tawny brown. Despite Nina's protest, I stored the owl in our freezer for later study. Nina imagined macabre scenes of my forgetting the cadaver and our landlords mistakenly defrosting it the next summer.

"Yes, our freezers were always stocked with birds and animals," Kristi said. "Some people find it morbid. But death can teach you a lot about life."

As I drove away, I replayed the image of Kristi in my mind's eye: out in the snow, fiercely dragging the Christmas tree as she crutched along. I thought of the stubborn independence of the Hays. Having done things one way for sixty years or so, they weren't about to stop anytime soon.

I'd wanted to ask Kristi about those first hard "frontier" years on the Cape, but it felt too forward. John had told me that Aiken, with his drinking and occasional cruelty and tendency to blurt out whatever came into his mind, had made Kristi wary. She perhaps hadn't bargained on living next to a wild drunken poet and raising her kids on an underpopulated sandbar. While John was slowly finding his voice and his calling in the landscape, how did she react to living on the Cape?

Kristi, I knew, had led a remarkable life of her own, along the way becoming a prominent local figure. She threw herself into helping John start up the Natural History Museum and became the head of the Brewster Ladies' Library in addition to raising three children. Despite the fact that she had made so much of her life, I couldn't help but feel a pang of empathy when I thought of her early days on "the dump" of Cape Cod. For Kristi, raised in Washington as the daughter of the director of the U.S. Lighthouse Service, there were no revelatory experiences at the herring run, and she might have been happier in a less remote place.

A family friend had told me a story about one of the Hays' early winters on Dry Hill. At the time John was frequently going to New York to do research for a book, and he always visited his mother in her brownstone on 37th Street. Kristi, left behind on the Cape, perhaps felt some resentment at this arrangement. In those days Brewster was truly remote, and power outages were frequent. Once when John was in New York the power went out for a particularly long, cold stretch. That night Kristi kept the kids warm with a roaring fire. The next day she called up John at his mother's. "If you don't get back here in twenty-four hours," she told him, "I'm going to start burning the furniture." She sounded like she meant it.

In December I began sending out applications for teaching jobs all over the country. I was doing this for the most unromantic and pedestrian of reasons: we needed the money. Over the previous few years I had often vowed that I, like John, would settle on Cape Cod forever, but this was becoming less and less likely. Nina and I had tried to buy a house, but the prices of real estate kept rising beyond our grasp. It was beginning to look like we would have to move to find new jobs and be able to afford a house.

John's life provided a stark contrast to ours. I was continually impressed by the simple fact that he had lived in the same place for more than half a century. Nina and I had moved from rental to rental since college. During our recent time back on Cape Cod, we had lived in beautiful houses, but every place we lived carried with it an unusual caveat: we had to leave during the summer. In the tourist season, our house on the edge rented for more than ten times what we paid during the off-season. It wasn't a bad setup, really, but it left us in a constant state of upheaval. Ours were temporary encampments. We never truly settled.

The more I moved around, the more stability and rootedness appealed to me, and in John I saw a parable of finding a place and rooting down. As much as I wanted to learn the story of John's life, it wasn't just facts I wanted. It seemed important to me to find out not just why he had come to Cape Cod but why he had stayed and what he had found.

With the winter solstice approaching, John and I took a walk to visit the abandoned osprey nest on the marsh on Chase Garden Creek. Though the land was flat enough, it was still a fairly challenging walk for an eighty-six-year-old man. But John said he was up for it.

"I haven't been out much lately due to my condition," he said when I arrived to pick him up.

"What condition?" I asked, falling for it.

"Old age," he said. He cracked a sly smile.

Despite his years, he didn't seem particularly old as we hiked the mile and a half to the nest. He was going without a cane, and seemingly without a problem. "I must be inspired by your youth," he joked.

Of course, the delight he now felt had been preceded by a good half-hour of inspired grousing. Standard procedure, I was learning. It had begun right when I picked him up. After he lowered himself into the Civic, he started in with a jeremiad that would have made Jeremiah blush. "There is no such thing as *home* in this country any longer" was how today's tirade had begun. Once he built up a full head of steam, damning the government and trophy homes and developers and most of all that great bugaboo "progress," there was nothing I could do but nod and agree. He was, of course, preaching to the choir. It was as if a two-man revival meeting were taking place in the little bubble of my Honda, my chorus of *uh-huhs* gradually sounding more and more like *amens*.

"We are turning out a nation of illiterates," he said on the way over. "We get our culture from the TV set. George Bush said the other day that he liked reading books just like the rest of us. So many nice pictures." He laughed at his own joke. Then it was back to today's lecture. *There is no home in America today. People have lost their sense of connection to place.*

What separated John's grumbling from that of an old man on the porch yelling at kids to keep their damn Wiffle ball off his lawn? Intelligence, insight, articulation. But there was no denying it was of the same genre. The world had gotten worse, and it was never that great to begin with.

But that was the human world. After a half-hour or so he had blown his pipes clean, and by the time we were deep in the woods he was truly relaxed. When we stopped to listen as a cardinal shot out its upward whittling notes, he seemed nothing short of ecstatic. "He's really letting it rip," he said.

As a rule, being away from houses and cars made John happier, but as we wound through the woods I felt the need to mention that we would soon be cutting across a road. "We have to walk through a neighborhood up ahead," I warned him.

"A neighborhood of birds or people?"

"People."

"Too bad," he said, shaking his head.

When we did reach the road, it was lined with half-built condos, and he studied it in mock awe. "Ah-ha," he said. "We've come upon a settlement."

As we dipped back into the woods, we talked about a strange recent change that had come over the Cape. People no longer built their own homes or even had their homes built for them. Instead, homes were built by developers before there were specific people to fill them. Of course, the people always came.

"It all goes back to the fact that so many people have been uprooted," John said. "That's the real story of the last century. Dispos-session. Starting with World War I and World War II and the con-stant wars afterward. With each one the technology has improved and the population has grown. And so people are on the run every-where. They barely settle before they are on the move again. As if they didn't know where they lived."

I knew him well enough now to understand that he was in par-ticularly high spirits. "Give me health and a day and I will make the pomp of the emperors ridiculous," wrote Emerson, and that seemed to be about all John required, at least today. Health problems had be-gun to plague him and Kristi, but if only he could have enough days like this one, it seemed to me, everything would be fine. I thought of something Deborah Diamond, the librarian from the Natural History Museum who was transcribing John's papers, had said to me: "With someone almost ninety, the tendency is to think of them in the past tense. But the amazing thing is how present John is."

At the marsh he lay down flat on his back, not bothering with the fact that the tide was coming in. Then he stretched his arms out and let the wetness of the peat soak up through him. This worried me; it was a warm December day, but it was still December. But he smiled widely and looked ready to sink down into the marsh and disappear completely. It was a smile of delight at his surroundings: the spartina grass, the soughing cattails, the blue sky above. A smile that said, *This is where I belong.*

After a while he sat up and stared at the shaggy abandoned osprey nest I had taken him there to see. Earlier, in the car, I had told him about our difficulties in trying to find a home. He'd warned me about settling on Cape Cod, saying that for all its beauty, it was being developed beyond recognition. "Even with the conservation land, one feels cooped up on the Cape," he had said. "Too crowded. Too many people who really don't live here. In the old days there was circulation and community."

But now he reconsidered. He spread his arms to indicate the world of the marsh, and by implication the Cape as well. "This place is so wonderful," he said quietly. "I suppose if you can find places like this, then it might still be worth living here."

The wind off the water blew through the reeds, and a kingfisher rattled by, the plane of its body at an upward incline, as if it were flying toward the moon and not its hollowed tunnel of a nest. I helped John to his feet, and we walked closer to the osprey nest. Ospreys are hopeless scavengers, and this was the most garbage-filled of the nests I regularly observed during the summers, the walls three feet high and stuffed with boat line and plastic and trash. The use of DDT after the war had meant that John had seen very few Cape ospreys until recent years. I pointed to the nest and recited much of what I'd learned about the birds over the years, happy to play the teacher for once, not the student.

As we walked back toward the woods, away from the marsh, John mentioned the different birds that he had studied during his travels around the world. "I was fascinated by the frigate birds I saw in Belize," he said.

"It's called the magnificent frigate bird now," I said, showing off a little.

"Yes," he agreed, "it's been upgraded."

The corners of his mouth turned up in that slightly childlike way they did when he made a joke. He was almost fifty years older than I was, and I sometimes thought that the generation gap was also a humor gap. Though he had never given me any indication that he was deaf, I always spoke loudly around him, and I often overemphasized my words in an unsubtle manner. But now I laughed easily. "Good one," I said.

It occurred to me that during our last couple of meetings I had begun to regard John less as a subject, more as a friend. He stopped suddenly and gave me his enigmatic look—a look I was beginning to know well—his sky-blue eyes intent below upward-shooting eyebrows.

"Without connection to a place," he said quietly, "we exile ourselves."

This was not like his earlier diatribe, but the obverse. Turned inside out and made positive, it sounded less like grumbling than wisdom.

"A lot of people dispossess themselves. That's what I'm trying to write about now. They lose a belief in anything outside of themselves. That is a terrifying possibility. The only thing that holds it all together is belief, after all."

He bent down and cocked his ear to the ground. "The only way of knowing where you live is being with the original inhabitants.

Think of how so many of the Cape's place-names are Indian names. We live on their bones. If you listen hard, you can hear mysterious voices rising from the earth. Listen."

This was accompanied by a sly, half-silly smile, but it was also more than half serious.

We listened for a while and then walked away from the marsh together, shoulder to shoulder. The back of John's pants and shirt was dark with marsh muck and water. As we followed the path, I held in my head the picture of him lying there on the spartina grass as if sinking into the earth. Flat on his back, he had looked ready to give himself up and begin the slow process of decay, becoming part of the cycle he had spent his life writing about. I imagined John Hay edging toward compost, imagined his body collapsing down into the peat. He had looked comfortable there, sinking into the familiar earth. And, I couldn't help but think, he had looked perfectly at home.

In *The Abstract Wild,* Jack Turner writes:

> What we need now is a new tradition of the wild that teaches us how human beings live best by living in and studying the wild without taming it or destroying it . . .
>
> It is a tradition we need to recreate for ourselves, borrowing when necessary from native cultures, but making it new—a wild tradition of our own.

A wild bunch is forming, an eclectic tribe returning to the wild to study, learn, and express. From them we will learn the lore, myth, literature, art, and ritual we so require. Frank Craighead, John Haines, and Gary Snyder are among the elders of this tribe.

To which, of course, I would add the name John Hay.

In fact, as we walked toward the car from the marsh, I made a confession to this effect. Looking back, it was an embarrassing moment, hopelessly unhip and earnest of me. But I couldn't help myself. When I'd begun recording John's voice back in September, I had done so, I hoped, with something close to objectivity. But my meetings with John had changed. In so-called primitive cultures, elders served multiple purposes: initiators, dispensers of tribal wisdom, and living examples of that wisdom. How was that so different from what John had done for so many people on Cape Cod? How was it so different from what he was doing for me?

A few days before our trip to the osprey nest, I had run into Deborah Diamond at the Natural History Museum. "The other day John gave me Mircea Eliade's book on shamanism," she had told me. "That's what I feel he is. A shaman."

At the time I'd felt like rolling my eyes. I couldn't picture John out in his studio wearing a buffalo head, eating mescaline, and rolling bones. But to some degree the word fit.

The ecological philosopher David Abrams writes that what defines a shaman is "the ability to slip out of the perceptual boundaries that demarcate his or her particular culture—boundaries reinforced by social customs, taboos, and, most importantly, the common speech of language—in order to make contact with, and learn from, the other powers in the land. His magic is precisely this heightened receptivity to the meaningful solicitations—songs, cries, gestures—of a larger, more-than-human field."

By this definition, who was to say that John wasn't practicing a sort of disciplined magic? I wasn't ready to call him a shaman. He wasn't, by definition. But *something* was going on.

"It's a little embarrassing to say out loud, but I need to," I told him as we walked away from the nest. "Sometimes I feel like hanging around you is like hanging around a tribal elder."

Even as I spoke, I worried that my words sounded too reverent. But John stopped walking and looked carefully at me. His eyebrows stood at crazed attention.

"It's not embarrassing to me," he said. "I have no tribal culture, of course, though I wish I had. But passing on tradition is not exclusive to native culture. To some degree it *is* culture. The old pass on to the young."

He began walking again but then stopped and kicked at the dirt. He turned toward me and looked me in the eye. "If I were to give you one piece of advice, it would be this," he said. "Dig into this place."

This directly contradicted his earlier warning against settling on the Cape. I asked what he meant by "digging in," though to be honest I already had a pretty good idea.

"When I first came here, I dug around a lot. Literally. It all started when I found an arrowhead in the garden—a fine quartz birdpoint. Of course, there weren't many artifacts up on my hill, because there was no water up there. But there was a fellow who lived around here named Charles Rennie, who collected hundreds of arrowheads. It pleased me that this land had been inhabited for thousands of years. I felt like I had found original ground. We lack both foresight and hindsight these days. We think our little inhabitation of four hundred years is really something. But we have a long way to go until we reach a tenth of the time the native people were here. When we arrived, the Wampanoags had already been living complex, interesting lives in this place for ten thousand years.

"One of the lies we like to tell ourselves, to ease our guilt, is that native people had no sense of property. This is preposterous, of course. They may have had a more fluid sense, but for hundreds of years before we arrived the local sachems doled out property and had a very clear sense of where territories began and ended." He shook his head vigorously before continuing.

"To broaden our minds. Now there's a wonderful phrase. One way to broaden your mind is by trying to understand different species from your own. But you can also broaden it by trying to understand different times, different epochs."

I mentioned Jack Turner's idea of borrowing from native cultures to create our own tradition of the wild.

"I don't know how we can wed Native American attitudes toward nature with our own," he said. "Our attitudes always get in the way—

two different ways of looking at nature. The Native Americans sought things out more clearly. When you say that, people assume you are romanticizing a lost way of life, but that's not it at all. People don't realize that the Indians were also very rigorous. It isn't easy, you know, to learn about the natural world. It takes sweat and intense concentration, and the quieting of the buzzing of our minds. During the ritual of the night chant of the Navaho, for instance, the communicant endures a lot to learn nature's ways. The ceremony lasts for eight days and nights, and unless you behave correctly, you're off the track. The moon, the sun, the stars, Mother Earth. How to align yourself with these? It takes work.

"What is nature? The originator. *Origins.* That got me interested in Indian life as well. When I taught at Dartmouth, I had a student named Gemma Lockhart, and we became very close. Her mother was a Lakota Sioux. She helped me understand something about tribal cultures, though I still don't understand much."

From my reading, I knew that Gemma Lockhart had set up a meeting between John and Fools Crow, a respected elder of her tribe. John had traveled to the Badlands of South Dakota to meet with Fools Crow, whom he described as "a grave old man with a look of unshakeable dignity and faith." Of the visit John wrote:

Through prayer too, Fools Crow said, one makes things happen. Prayer joins the visible to the invisible world. It makes us communicants in the universe, part of all that lives. I also asked him about thunder beings, which I had heard of before in this land of seasons punctuated by thunder and lightning.

"They," he said, "are spirits of our dead ancestors. They live beyond the thunder, and are consulted by prayer."

I thought I was hearing distant echoes in his speech of a very ancient culture, praying, singing, dancing before the Great Mystery.

The visit had a great impact on John, and inspired a period of deepening studies of Native Americans. I asked him if he was still in touch with Gemma.

"Yes, I am," he said. "Now she's trying to do a documentary, but we're very unclear about what she wants to do. I don't know how to help her. Fools Crow is dead. But she's got a man named Eagle Bear out there, and Eagle Bear is supposed to be giving her counsel. Gemma visited me recently, during the time the Brant geese were down at the beach. Sometimes they come in great numbers, as you know, sometimes very few. She would get up every morning before dawn with her heavy camera equipment and head down to the beach to film. I told her I'd try to help her with the documentary, but I'm not sure how I can. As I say, I have no tribal culture myself."

He stopped again and stared off into the woods. He spoke very slowly. "We just don't understand the sort of behavior that puts nature first. It's what will be the end of us. We think, 'We've got it, man'; we think, 'We've gone past the moon.' But if all we do is find one desert after another, then what's all this crap about conquering space? It's here that matters. That's all we've got. I looked at that line again in Frost the other day: 'Earth's the right place for love. I don't know where it's likely to go better.' A lovely line. And damn true."

"It seems astonishing that the old varied culture of the American Indian, which had an intimate, alive, spiritual connection with all nature on this continent, should have almost completely vanished," John wrote in 1969.

In this cynical age, the thought of an old white guy feeling kinship with aboriginal peoples is sure to bring snickers. And to some, the idea of this kinship might seem suspect, even comical. When I lived in the West, I went to hear the writer Sherman Alexie speak. Alexie is a Native American who has been critical of white people for romanticizing "Indian ways." If there is something refreshingly challenging about this, briskly sweeping out easy New Age spiritualism, it is also reductionist. It neglects the fact that throughout history, pilgrims and searchers have always looked to cultures other than their own, often older cultures, to inform and enrich their lives. To cut off conversations between cultures is to cut off part of the world. And what could be more natural for those who are trying to root down into their own land than to look back at the earliest inhabitants of that land?

Still, I agree with Alexie to some extent: a dogmatic adoration of all things native is useless. It is natural to romanticize what has been lost, so to us the lost cultures of native peoples shine with the sheen of the romantic. But the simple fact is that they are also worthy of study and emulation. For one thing, as a people Native Americans lived as part of nature. This may have not been entirely by choice: they were limited by technology, and if they hadn't been limited, they might have chosen a different way. But whatever the reasons, they did live closer to the wild than we do. And so they had to learn the world of rocks and trees and seasonal movement and migration, because their lives depended on such knowledge. This may not make the Wampanoags or the Nausets perfect creatures, but it can give direction to those of us who consciously attempt to bring our own lives closer to the natural world. This is not romantic but practical. We can't recreate native spiritualism, and we shouldn't try, but we can find in it hints of what we need: ritual, close daily encounters with nature, a recognition of the sacredness of place, an openness to the worlds of plants and animals.

John Hay had long ago chosen a different route from that of his immediate ancestors, and more and more he looked back to the first Americans. His love of the native peoples began well before the neo-primitivism that started coming into vogue in the 1960s. During the Eisenhower years he was already wrestling with a lifestyle quite different from those around him: more radical, a concept of life and survival tied to the land, an intimacy with local plants and animals, and a sense of the importance of ritual and a spiritual connection to place. And he had put his money where his mouth was, so to speak. John had turned his back not so much on success as on the contemporary definitions of success. "Nature is no longer my hobby," he said in 1961, "it's my life."

Maybe Deborah Diamond wasn't so far off after all. Wasn't it a fairly shamanistic enterprise to spend your life learning the particulars of your place while throwing yourself into the lives of the fish and birds? "Of course I can only write distantly about the original inhabiters," John admitted. But something not just about their lives but about their great losses at the hands of "progress" struck a chord in him. Perhaps both John's intimacy with nature and his feeling for the loss of nature could help him empathize with the country's original people to a degree that most of us can't. It would be a disservice to the Native Americans' historical plight to compare their loss of life, land, and sacred space to the destruction of Cape Cod by commercialism and development that John had witnessed. But as John's writing pointed out, what had happened centuries ago was still happening today—the steady driving out of what seemed to him most sacred in the name of profit. "We came as conquerors," he said. "And to a large degree conquerors we remain."

He saw those who lived here long ago not as mere romantic relics but as possible role models. And what did these role models teach? That a life intertwined with nature was not just more balanced and healthier and other such dull things. That it was also more *exciting*. Nature was the source, not just of life but of creativity, of exuberance, and, not least of all, of self-knowledge.

"The American Indian saw the Word behind all manifested things, the primal, creative power," he wrote. "The Word was invoked through silence and dreams, through chants in healing ceremonies and hypnotic poetry that mirrored the sounds of nature ... Nature undefined is what I know in myself."

John believed that there are still ways to get back to that older way of being. Through empathy, through imagination, through art. And of course through nature itself. Nature, to John, was the undiscovered country.

Obviously, John Hay wasn't the only person who had come to Cape Cod and become interested in "digging things up." Hundreds of scientists, artists, historians, fishermen, farmers, writers, and archaeologists have discovered a ground rich with the humus of past human occupation. Their motivations have all been mixed, but they have all wanted, to some degree, to learn their place and to find something below the thin skein of the present.

"Dig in," John Hay told me. What had he hoped to find with all his digging? It certainly wasn't dry relics like "history" and "tradition." Like Thoreau, he wanted us to "wedge our feet downward through the slush and mud of opinion, and prejudice, and tradition, and delusion, and appearance." Thoreau, of course, was more of a traditionalist than he cared to admit, and one of the traditions he relied on was the native one, which helped him in his attempts to connect to his place. The goal of John Hay's digging was similar: to wedge downward and find what he called "original ground."

Maybe one of the things that John was digging around for was hints of how to be in the world. Maybe he was hoping to find a living use of tradition, a way to put things to use. And maybe it wasn't just hints that he was looking for but a sign that he was on the right road. After all, with the possible exception of Thoreau, there were really few precedents in his own society for a person to spend years shedding his skin and throwing himself out into the lives of herring or terns. Perhaps what he was seeking in native cultures was some confirmation of alternative ways, a culture that valued what he had come to value. In the end, maybe it wasn't so crazy that John Hay saw native people who lived closer to the land as examples of how to live.

And by choosing to live this way, he had unwittingly provided an example for those, like Gemma Lockhart and me and many others, who came after him. Gemma called John an "arrow-shooter," an elder who showed others how they might live better in the world. He was part of what Jack Turner called the "new tradition of the wild," one of the elders of that tribe who could pass down not just knowledge but values. Of course I would never live as close to the wild as native peoples did, or even, in all likelihood, as John Hay did. But it seemed to me that it was the effort in that direction that mattered, the attempt. For me, walking out to the bluff every day with my eyes open had become a way to begin moving outside myself and into another world, and I found that private changes occurred when I walked. It might not have been a monumental transformation. But it was a start.

After spending time with John, I also found that I was becoming less afraid to explore certain ideas that I'd been skeptical of. For instance, I'd always known of the work of Gary Snyder, but as winter closed in, I began to read it. Snyder had mirrored John's attempts to wedge downward. He, like John, had to some extent turned his back on the world to root down into his chosen place, in his case a hundred-acre plot of woodlands in the Sierra Nevadas in California that he called Kitkitdizze, a native word for a common ground cover. Snyder and his family built their own home soon after they moved to the land in 1970, and during those early years they had no running water or electricity. Part of what Snyder learned over the years at Kitkitdizze was the importance of "imaginative descent" through the layers of time. Ed Folsom wrote of how Snyder defied the closure of the American frontier "by descending: if the Indians are no longer to be found across a geographical frontier, Snyder will seek them out across a psychic frontier, make an imaginative descent rather than a physical journey." Snyder wrote: "We have a western white history of a hundred and fifty years; but when we look at a little bit of American Indian folklore, myth, read a tale, we're catching just a tip of the iceberg of forty or fifty thousand years of human experience, on this continent, in this place." Snyder's lofty aim is no less than a reinhabiting of America, and at his most optimistic he sees Kitkitdizze as just "one tiny node in an evolving net of bioregional homesteads and camps."

If that is the case, then Dry Hill is another node in the net. And it is heartening that Snyder, the Zen poet, born in the Pacific Northwest, and the Cape Cod writer, born in Manhattan, have found similar ground after years of wedging downward. "We have not yet discovered America," John had written long ago, and discovering America was still the work ahead. Those who come later and attempt to continue that discovery and descent will of course disagree about some of the techniques and reach different conclusions. That doesn't matter. In fact, to a certain extent the names of these forerunners and "arrow-shooters" doesn't matter. There are many such elders, and on a larger scale the individual isn't the point; what matters is the movement toward digging in and discovering America. For those who come after, these elders provide something valuable that they themselves never had. They give us maps to show where original ground might be found, and tools to dig with. They give us a wild tradition.

"It's all a loss," John said to me as we hiked through the woods. "In the face of all our losses, it's difficult to face and retain optimism. I have watched what was best about Cape Cod be defiled in my lifetime. But optimism is necessary, despite what we are doing to the earth. It's a tool. We need it to keep going."

The comment was in response to my telling him that another copse of woods in Brewster was now under threat from development. I was coming to learn that John took the destruction of trees very personally. "It is an unfortunate man or woman who has never loved a tree," he had once written. As a child he had had a particularly close relationship with a stand of white pines in New Hampshire and had been stung when that stand was uprooted by the hurricane of 1938. Of the hurricane's aftermath he wrote: "My father, who loved trees, came up from New York where he was working to view the damage, sat down by the side of the road, and cried."

Perhaps it was because of a hereditary sensitivity, or perhaps because he had known Cape Cod when it was barren, but John couldn't stand to see the Cape's trees uprooted. "Have you seen what they've done to that stand of old cedars off Main Street?" he'd asked earlier in the walk. "It's a massacre. There's a huge pile of sawdust. Like blood."

I thought about John's tirades over the fate of Cape Cod and decided that they, too, were mostly expressions of pain. But if there had been much pain in fighting his lifelong losing battle against development, there was also something ennobling about his willingness to be vulnerable. He had started the Cape Cod Museum of Natural History, and he had worked tirelessly to educate children about nature and battled throughout his life to save land on the Cape. And he had walked the shores for years, trying to save shorebirds covered in oil that had spilled or been discharged from ships. All winter long he would patrol the beaches, searching for eiders, scoters, auks, loons, and old-squaws with feathers that shined "sickeningly, with a heavy coating of oil." He wrote articles in the local papers that instructed others on how to take care of the oiled birds they found: "Warmth is the first necessity ... Bathe the bird in lukewarm water, keeping soap out of its eyes ...

Keep the birds in boxes lined with dried salt hay, seaweed, or some other absorbent material."

John still had some of the old family reserve, but his passion for other creatures let him break through. In an essay called "The Dovekie and the Ocean Sunfish," he tells the story of coming upon an oil-covered dovekie, a small seabird that the waves had flung against the rocks:

> I picked it up, and what a trembling there was in it, what a whirring heart! I carried it back to the car, thinking to clean the oil off later and see if I could bring it back to health, always a precarious job. But after a few minutes in the heated car the bird's blood began to flow from its breast, to my great dismay, and there seemed to be little I could do about it. I began to feel like a terrible meddler and a coward. With that I took it back to calmer waters, on the bay side of the Cape, and let it go without illusions about the cruel mother that might take care of it better than I, but I felt my fruitless attempts to save it would be worse... That bird, which had bloodied me and been so close and warm in my hand, left me on the beach to shake with the weight of human ignorance.

John's encounter with the bird encompassed both his eagerness to save what was being lost and his increasing vulnerability to those losses. But more than that, it seemed to me an example of the way that his emotional world had become intertwined with the natural world, almost to the point where they were inseparable. As painful as this intertwining was, it also was, in the end, a hopeful thing, for without the deep emotional connection, who could ever lift a hand to fight against the losses? Or, just as important, why would anyone? The answer, for John, was that fighting, though against his nature, had become imperative. Over the years he had begun to develop what Jack Turner calls "the reciprocity between the wild in nature and the wild in us." And this reciprocity stirred his essentially apolitical nature to action. Like his father crying for the downed trees, he felt a visceral connection.

And this, I began to think as I spent more time with John, was the only way to really fight for the world that was being lost. Not being a joiner myself, I had always chafed against environmentalism— against any ism, for that matter. But John's life suggested a much more radical route than sending money to Greenpeace. It suggested that we can only fight back when we feel the world's joy, which also means feeling the world's pain, on a personal level. And to feel that, the connective tissue between self and world has to grow so tight that they become one.

5

AN ELEMENTAL LIFE

John and I made plans for another December outing, but they fell through when he became sick. Then his family arrived for the holidays and Christmas activities crowded both of our schedules. My contact with John during that time was secondhand, mostly through my talks with Deborah Diamond. Deborah had become all but indispensable to John, not just as an archivist, filer, transcriber, and reader but as a friend, chauffeur, and organizer of his life.

"In his journals he is always philosophizing directly about life," she said when I visited her at the Cape Museum of Natural History. "But in the books he puts these things into the minds of terns and turtles and alewives."

We stood on opposite sides of the checkout desk at the museum library and talked about John for almost an hour. Deborah was visiting him every week, helping type things up and gathering the mouse-eaten manuscripts from the studio closet. With his vision problems,

John relied on her, and in turn Deborah had begun to rely on him. In the natural world their relationship would have been described as one of mutualism. Clearly Deborah's visits were becoming the most exciting part of her weeks, and just as clearly, John would have been lost without her.

"I feel like he's the source," she told me, laughing. "He's mythological, like the Fisher King."

I admitted there was something mythical about traveling up that long driveway to see the wise man on the hill. Deborah's enthusiasm was infectious, as was her laugh. It had a birdlike quality, yodeling delightfully like the calls of the loons I heard on the bay after a storm. Sometimes her ideas seemed a bit too mystical for my taste, but her affection for John ran deep.

"It sounds silly, but it's the best thing about my life," she said. "If I lose this job at the museum, it's okay. I feel that the purpose of this job was to give me contact with John. When you're around him, you know you're experiencing something outside yourself. John gets that in nature. It's interesting to me that he's come to personify the exact thing he seeks in nature. Something beyond himself. That's the biggest thing that I've learned from him. You become what you observe. You become what you value. And if anyone will teach you that lesson, it's John. That's why I don't think he is a personal writer at all. He has become what he is observing. He *is* the mystery. And that's his greatest gift."

"He'd get nervous if he heard you talking about him this way," I said.

"He has heard me talk this way. I say it right to him. And he just looks at me with that little smile and says, 'Interesting.' And then he'll slap his hands together and say, 'Okay, let's get back to work.'"

She told me about the recent spate of interest in John. A biographer of his grandfather had called and insisted on booking a flight from LA to visit him, despite John's warning that he would respond only "through the post." And several newspapers had called, and there had even been talk of a documentary. John was suddenly hot, and it unnerved him. "Now that I'm almost dead, they're suddenly interested," he had grumbled to Deborah. "They want to feed on my corpse."

Deborah smiled. "He's secretly thrilled, of course," she said.

After Christmas I tried to invite John and Kristi over to dinner, but it proved too complicated. I missed my frequent meetings with John and was anxious to see him again. In late December I'd interviewed with a couple of schools, and I felt my time on Cape Cod was running out. In January I dropped by a few times to take up the mail, but I didn't want to exhaust him with questions or tempt him with a walk.

Finally, in the middle of January, John invited me over for a real visit. We'd had some snow, and though the roads were clear on the drive over, the long driveway, shaded by the canopy of trees, was packed with glazed snow and ice. In fact, Dry Hill seemed to exist in an entirely different, and more wintry, microclimate from the rest of Brewster and Dennis.

Kristi greeted me, and I was surprised when she told me that John was out, having made the trek to get the mail "over the hill." He must have been cutting through on one of his trails when I drove up, but a look at the hill suggested it would best be traversed going down by Flexible Flyer, going up by snowshoes. She invited me in, and we sat in the kitchen. Kristi was still getting around with two crutches, one for each arm. A schnauzer named Deuce, a Christmas gift from the kids, raced around her ankles.

I told Kristi about the pictures I'd seen of her and John with the Aikens, how young and dashing they all looked.

"Eons ago," she said, but smiled.

At first I thought she was smiling bashfully, looking down at the ground, but then she explained that she had recently had eye troubles. Because of John's failing vision, she had been reading him a biography of John Adams at night, but now she couldn't see either. For the first time in their lives, they both went to bed without reading.

"It's been a hard year," I said.

"The hardest. Ever since I fell last November, it's one thing after another."

I would have enjoyed talking to Kristi longer, but suddenly John, dressed for Arctic exploration, burst in with the mail.

When Kristi asked him how the walk had been, he said, "Fine," but then, alone with me on our way up to the studio, he admitted he had fallen. "On my ass," he said, slapping himself to indicate both the place and his ongoing hardiness. The icy path to the studio seemed only a little less dangerous than the trip down the hill, but John, half blind and now bruised, charged right up it.

When I expressed my concern about the conditions, he cut me off. "I'm not going to let them keep me locked up inside," he said. "If I do, then I might as well be dead. I need to get out and talk to the trees and birds."

We knocked the snow off our shoes and went into the studio. Then we settled into our usual seats across from each other. John crossed his arms and looked up at the ceiling, preparing to leave the present behind. Talking about the past always relaxed him; it was so much easier than now, so much clearer and more vivid.

He spoke, as he so often did when he looked backward, about Conrad Aiken, about his elevated speech and his elevated life. "The thing about Conrad was that he truly pontificated. His language was quite beautiful. No one wants 'fancy talk' anymore, but I find myself missing it. Sometimes now when I'm alone in the woods, I start quoting Shakespeare. Not to impress anyone—who would I impress? The squirrels?—but just to hear the beautiful language."

He stood abruptly and set to fiddling with the heater, finally banging it with the flat of his hand. It coughed to life, and he turned and focused on me.

"Why don't more of us try consciously to elevate our lives? That's a question that interests me. Laziness? Fear? It seems to me that we are in the midst of a crisis of empathy. We lack empathy for other species, other cultures, other peoples. This isn't very grown-up of us. You can say what you want about Conrad, but he was always attempting to stretch his mind. He was daring. He didn't accept some old mode of being. He wanted to explore this miraculous life in a way that was distinctly his. You can't say that of many people."

John spoke about Conrad for another twenty minutes or so; some of what he said I had heard before, some I hadn't. Then he began to talk wistfully about his father, Clarence. After a while longer, he excused himself to go mark his territory on the side of the studio.

A minute after he disappeared around the corner of the studio, Kristi appeared. Eye trouble and bad back be damned—she had double-caned her way up the icy path to find out when we would be finished. I had a strange thought: maybe she was a little jealous of my spending all this time with John. But she also had a more practical motive: someone had to walk Deuce.

When John circled back around, she asked him if he was returning to the house.

"Not this moment," he said. "I've got to put myself back together again. We'll be done soon. But maybe Dave has another question or two."

Actually, I didn't, but Kristi said fine and began making her way down the toboggan trail to the house. I asked if I could give her a hand, but she called over her shoulder again that she was fine. These weren't easy people to help.

Before we closed up the studio, John turned to me with a grim expression. He had been turning over something in his mind, and now he said it out loud.

"It's hard not to imagine that we are at the end of something," he said. "Hard not to imagine that we have forgotten something about how humans have always existed on this earth. Nature has never been some separate thing off in a box. Nature has always been us, intermingled with us, intertwined. You have to wonder how long we can survive, cradling the illusion that we are something separate."

With that he closed the studio door and we hiked down to the house. It was dark now, and the path was even icier, but John still refused my offer of an arm. Before I left, I asked if I could walk the dog, and to this they agreed. Kristi handed me the leash and I clipped it on Deuce's collar. "You'll be knighted if he craps," John said.

I headed out the door, but at the last moment John decided to join me for his second walk of the day. He pulled on his coat and hat again.

"Are you walking me or the dog?" he asked as we made our way cautiously down the driveway. I wondered, too: I again felt like grabbing his arm to steady him.

After we had walked for twenty minutes or so, John deemed the journey a "half success," as Deuce managed to piss but not crap. Back in the house, we freed the dog and began to unbundle. This was always the point where I would thank John and Kristi and be on my way. But I didn't feel like going yet. I'd listened to John wax eloquent about cocktail hour with Aiken often enough—"the communion of all friendly minds separated in time and in space"—and while I didn't expect to be served the ceremonial gin in one of Aiken's sacred chalices, I at least hoped to throw back one of the good beers I'd noticed in the Hay pantry. And so I invited myself in for a drink.

"I suppose it's late enough," John said. "It's past five."

"It's a wonderful idea," said Kristi. "Please do come in."

We were soon seated around the kitchen table. Kristi reached back and opened the fridge door with one of her crutches. She grabbed a corked bottle of white wine while John and I drank beer, he a Dos Equis, I a Sam Adams. We toasted to the new year's being better than the last one. And to the return of good health. Then I told them that something of the expression in the eye of the drawing of Sam Adams on the bottle always reminded me of my father.

"Good lord," said John. "Seeing Clarence every time I drank!"

"When my father died," I said, "we took his ashes on a little trip." I described how my family had taken my father's boat out to spread his remains on Cape Cod Bay. We had rigged it with lines so that his urn could sit in the captain's seat and steer the boat out beyond the bluff to the Sears beach. We placed a Miller Lite beside the urn. My father had been an accomplished man, but he had always had a taste for both booze and the absurd. Like Aiken, he was a burly, thick-necked man who enjoyed holding court over drinks late into the night.

"He sounds like a good man," John said. "The kind of man we used to have around here before everybody was from someplace else. Was he a naturalist?"

I laughed out loud. "No, but he loved birds," I said. I decided to leave out the fact that he especially loved watching his cats hunt those birds at our feeder.

My story of the ashes led John to tell a story that I had heard before. Just after they met, Conrad asked John to drive to New Bedford with him to pick up the ashes of his uncle Alfred, once the librarian of Harvard College. John, the shy young apprentice, had been "deputized" to carry the ashes in his lap all the way back to Cape Cod.

If I'd heard the story before, Kristi had probably heard it at least a hundred times; still, she didn't say anything. I noticed that she was the kind of listener whose ready expression encourages talk. She had a tolerant way of letting John indulge in a monologue for a while before pulling him in.

As for me, I was so excited just to be part of the famous cocktail tradition—even if it was a little diminished from former glorious times —that I nearly finished my second beer by the time John had drunk half of his. While we drank, Kristi talked for a while about growing up in Washington as the daughter of the director of lighthouses. She mentioned that Amelia Earhart was a distant aunt and early hero. Then she described having once met Eleanor Roosevelt: "I was just a teenager, and my youth group hosted an event in Washington that she attended. Mrs. Roosevelt was late—she was always late, I'd heard. I was anxious about meeting her and had my head down at the desk, and she came up behind me and patted me on the shoulder. 'Don't you worry, dear,' she said to me very gently. I'll never forget that."

We went on in this way for an hour or so, taking turns recollecting, while Kristi drank another half-glass of wine and John nursed his beer. Then I had a surprise for them. I went out to the car to get the copy of Conrad Aiken's letters that I had bought at Parnassus. Once back inside, I opened to the page I'd marked and read out loud from a section I had discovered about Conrad's dream of Emily Dickinson and John on old Stony Brook Road. During the night of March 13, 1971, Conrad Aiken, then eighty-two, had had a dream. The next morning he described it in a letter:

> John Hay and I were walking down Stony Brook Road, as it used to be, and in the fields beside it, and one of us said, It must be here that Emily's apple orchard was. I looked down into the grass, and sure enough, there it was—rows of tiny apple trees, two inches high, each with a little red apple, size of a cranberry, on top, and I at once plucked one and popped it in my mouth, where I began to peel the skin off with tongue and teeth. As I did so, the taste of the little apple turned itself into language, in fact a poem, which went—
>
> > Human, thou tastest
> > Now in me
> > A breath of
> > Immortality
> > I planted with my hands
> > This tree
> > And now
> > I give it back to thee.

When I was done, John remarked on the line about the taste of the apple turning into language. "I never heard that before," he said, which surprised me.

Kristi nodded and said it was lovely. While John was enjoying himself, Kristi seemed to be having the most fun.

"We talk about the old days all the time," she said when I finally made my way to the door. "But not usually such *old* old days."

I said goodnight and walked out to my car. Snow shone white on either side of the driveway as I drove down Dry Hill. "They're like characters from some old novel," Deborah had said to me, and I'd nodded in agreement. Living on top of their mythic hill, still managing to enjoy the present but fed more and more by the secret spring of memory. After they were gone, the land would pass into conservation, and there would be no more like them. As I pulled out of the driveway and onto the road, I had the distinct impression that I was leaving behind a different and older world.

It had been so nice to socialize with both John and Kristi that I decided to try again to invite them over for dinner. I'd mentioned the idea to Kristi that evening in their kitchen. "I'd love to see the water from your house," she said. We decided to wait a couple of weeks so that Kristi's eyes could get better, and scheduled a dinner party for January 25. Nina and I were nervous about the meal, of course. I considered grilling, but we finally decided on a roast, which seemed like the kind of thing you would make for people in their eighties.

On the Friday of the dinner party we cleaned the house and Nina marinated the roast. The phone rang in the early afternoon. John was calling to say that Kristi wasn't feeling well and they would not be coming after all. Naturally we assumed that something more complex was occurring behind the scenes, but the fact was, we were sort of relieved.

It turned out that Kristi was more than a little sick. She would be in the hospital and in rehab on and off for close to two months. Over the next weeks the Hay children drove down from Maine to be with John in the house on the weekends, but he spent much of his time alone. It was hard to get a clear report of Kristi's diagnosis, and it was also hard to do things for John. He kept refusing my offers of help. He was living alone and eating Dinty Moore stew.

Deborah Diamond was one of the few people outside the family who could get close to him, and she reported that he wasn't doing well. Then the doctors told him that Kristi would have to go into a nursing home or get twenty-four-hour care at home.

"They're going to have to kill me before they put me in a home," John said. "And no one's going to move in with us."

"We're coming to the end of something," Deborah told me when I visited her at the library.

But then things took a sudden hopeful turn. By the second week of February, Kristi was stabilizing and had gone to rehab. "I just want to go home," she said to Deborah over the phone, and it soon looked like she would.

On Lincoln's birthday, Deborah and John celebrated by reading one of John Milton Hay's poems. They also laughed at a letter that a biographer of Lincoln had sent them. John's father, Clarence, had donated two of his father's copies of the Gettysburg Address to the Library of Congress in 1916. The Lincoln biographer, who hadn't done his homework regarding John's birth date, asked if John had any memories of the event. John began to mock-dictate a return letter to Deborah: "Ah yes, I remember the ceremony well. I was a one-year-old at the time and in diapers, but it was quite a memorable event..."

On the night of February 25, I called John again. He was in good spirits; Kristi was doing much better and was up and walking at the rehab center. I told him I was planning on driving to Eastham the next morning and then walking down the beach to the spot where Henry Beston's Outermost House had once stood. He was intrigued by the idea but worried about the weather. "I get my weather from one of these marine forecast machines with a voice like a robot," he said. "And the robot tells me a storm is coming in tonight."

Luckily, the robot was dead wrong. It was a clear night, with a ring around a nearly full moon. The next morning, the twenty-sixth, was one of the most freakishly warm days of a freakishly warm winter.

"I'll have to throw that robot on the scrap heap," John said when I called at nine. "Can you give me a half-hour? Deuce just crapped and I've got to clean it up."

By the time I got over to Dry Hill it felt like a day in mid-May. After inviting me into the house to look at a real estate listing for the latest "monstrosity"—"If you've got an extra million lying around, you can buy this"—we walked outside, and John pointed to the garden. "Crocuses in February. Red-winged blackbirds here all winter. All the other birds coming back sooner. The grass green. Everything is wrong, wrong, wrong. The signs are all wrong, and the world is out of whack. We never used to have turkey vultures stay through the winter. I suppose now, without the deep frosts, they can smell the carrion."

John looked old and tired. The winter had taken a lot out of him. I noticed the small blood vessels lining his face and his hair, uncut since Kristi went into the hospital, flowing long and white below the baseball cap.

I opened the door of the Civic's passenger side for him, but as usual he wouldn't let me help him into the car. We drove east and then north on Route 6A, toward the lower Cape, chatting all the way, moving easily from politics to jokes. I mentioned that I had recently met a man named Dick Hilmer, who ran a kayaking business at the Goose Hummock shop in Orleans and who took handicapped kids and poor kids from the city out on kayaking trips. Dick and I had gotten to talking, and he'd mentioned that John Hay had been his inspiration and mentor; one of the main reasons he had gone into his line of work.

"Well, it's very good to hear that," John said. "It's gratifying. Sometimes you feel like you're doing all this work and no one is noticing."

We drove for a while in silence, and then John mentioned that he had recently been sent a new anthology of nature writing. "It's a thousand pages, for god's sake. Do you think I'm ever going to read that? God bless them all. Hooray for us nature writers!"

"It's like anything else," I said. "There's more of us and less land. Overdevelopment."

We talked about various writers in the collection, starting with

Henry David Thoreau. I mentioned how Thoreau had supposedly become dulled toward the natural world once tuberculosis set in.

"Yes, the disease led to a lack of interest in his surroundings," he said. "Like some of the people over at Kristi's rehab center. Someone would be doing them a favor if they blew up their TVs. You've got to fight that with all your might. You have to retain interest in the physical world. Without the world, you are dead."

A while later we arrived at Coast Guard Beach, which had been the famous home of the man who could be considered John Hay's most obvious literary forebear. In 1926, Henry Beston built a small cabin a mile and a half south of the old Coast Guard station. He spent a year in the tiny, window-filled house perched on the edge of a dune less than a stone's throw from the Atlantic, and the result of that year was his classic book, *The Outermost House*. I asked John if he had read it when he was young.

"Of course," he said. "What American boy wouldn't want to read about a life of isolation in nature? Beston was a romantic, and he appealed to my romantic sense."

We parked behind the Coast Guard station and walked over to the guardrail overlooking Nauset Marsh. If the Atlantic had been Beston's front yard, the marsh had been his back, flooding from the west to make the spit of Coast Guard Beach into a thin peninsula. Today the marsh was flooded entirely. I had never seen it higher, and it looked as if the narrow arm of sand might be overrun on both sides.

"The full moon," John said as he cinched up his pants. "I came out here after the February storm of '78. The sea broke right through to the marsh and took the last of the cottages with it. I watched the houses bobbing in the marsh. They gradually sank, but for a while they bobbed along like small ships. Their windows looked like eyes."

One of those cottages had been Henry Beston's Outermost House. I remembered John's dream, the dream he had had upon first arriving on Cape Cod, of a house floating out on the sea. Finally, almost forty years after the dream, he had actually seen it. It had taken a while, but it was as if he had conjured it up.

Built in 1926, the Outermost House was moved several times over the years, always in retreat against the sea's advancement. In 1964, the house was dedicated as a national literary monument. One thousand people attended the dedication, including the governor, Secretary of the Interior Stewart Udall, a young Bob Finch, and a frail and ailing Henry Beston. Beston, seventy-six at the time and supported by his cane, read from the final section of his book. He began shakily but built up strength until, according to the *Worcester Telegram and Gazette*, "dozens of people were weeping."

"Whatever attitude to human existence you fashion for yourself, know that it is valid only if it be the shadow of an attitude toward Nature," he said that day. "A human life, so often likened to a spectacle on a stage, is more justly a ritual."

Beston had been understandably pleased with the recognition his house had received, but while the state had the authority to make the place a monument, the ocean, in the end, trumped the government. Fourteen years later the sea wrote the house's final chapter, dragging it out to sea while John Hay watched. Beston was dead by then, but his wife commented, "I think Henry would have said a great storm was the way it should go."

We walked down the boardwalk to the beach. I noticed that John was moving much more slowly than he had in the fall. But he was still appreciative of what he saw and stopped often to gaze out at the water. To those of us who lived on the bay side of the Cape, the outer beach always seemed a revelation. We stood facing the Atlantic with no land between us and Europe. The breakers rolled in with great sprays of white froth, kicking up halos of mist.

"Listen to that," John said. "What better noise? The plunge followed by the seethe."

The roar was steady, powerful, a great watery mantra like nothing we had on our tamer side of the Cape. Gulls dipped into the great troughs between the white foam. To our right, the south, the spit of sand we stood on extended down toward Orleans; to our left was Nauset Light and, below it, sharp clay cliffs half hidden in mist.

The temperature had climbed above sixty, but the wind kept us from taking our coats off. I had hoped to walk with John down to the site where Beston's house had once stood, but it was obvious he wouldn't be able to make it. He closed his eyes and smiled.

"*La mer,*" he said. "There is nothing like it. So invigorating. Beston must have slept well."

We walked closer to the surf and made a remarkable discovery.

The sea had kicked up its usual rubble, and among the shells and the seaweed was a workman's glove. The glove clutched a bunch of yellow flowers. "What a wondrous sight," said John. "A last gift from the sea."

It looked like a still life on the sand, and John stared at it as if examining a painting. After a while I said that I needed to head up into the dunes to find "the little boys' room."

"I'll stay down here," he said, waving his cane at the wildness of beach and ocean. "In the big boys' room."

When I returned, we looked out at the ocean for a half-hour, not moving or talking much. When we finally started heading back to the car, I mentioned that Beston hadn't thought very highly of Thoreau. "Beston said Thoreau wasn't warm enough and didn't have much heart," I said. "And that his book Cape Cod was dull."

"Well, of course Cape Cod is somewhat dull," John said. "It doesn't hold a candle to Walden."

"He seemed to think that Thoreau wasn't much of a naturalist. And made fun of him for doing his laundry at his mother's house and eating Mom's cherry pies."

"Well, there Beston was on poor footing. Thoreau noticed things. He was likely a better naturalist than Beston ever was. And as for going home on weekends, that has nothing to do with wildness. He was making the old mistake, confusing wildness with wilderness."

"There can be domestic wildness," I agreed.

We made our way back to the car and then drove along the coast to the Nauset lighthouse. John wanted to check the sea cliffs to see how much had been cut away since his last visit, in the fall. We kept staring out at the sea and mumbling the word *beautiful* and then laughing at our own inarticulateness. I mentioned that I had read a recent review of Robinson Jeffers's *Collected Poems* by someone who took Jeffers to task for using that same word—*beautiful*—too often.

"Ah yes, a high crime," John said. "I wonder if that reviewer has ever stepped outdoors."

A decade before Henry Beston retreated to the Eastham spit, Robinson Jeffers had done the same thing on Carmel Point in California, on a cliff overlooking the Pacific. Jeffers wrote that he lived at "continent's end," and I mentioned this to John.

"Which direction is the end of the world?" he said. "East or west? I suppose it depends which way you look. As long as you look out at the sea, you feel like you are on the edge. Beston and Jeffers were like two gunslingers walking off paces back to back across the country. One looking east over the Atlantic, the other west over the Pacific. But they both figured out how much the sea had to offer."

We climbed back into the car and headed south along the coast again. We drove in silence for a while. Then I mentioned that the director of the Natural History Museum had asked me if there was anything the museum could do to honor John.

"I'm past honors now," he said. "If he wants to do one thing for me, it would be getting rid of that damn punch clock he put in. It's a crime to have employees punching in and out at a museum of natural history. That clock is an affront to my sense of time. Cyclical time, natural time, ceremonial time. That's the kind of time a nature museum should run on."

"Maybe I can suggest a John Hay memorial punch clock ceremony," I said. "Where I take a sledgehammer to it."

"Now that I would gladly attend."

When we were halfway back to the Coast Guard station, I pulled over by the side of the road and we followed a path down to the edge of the cliff. The path wasn't clear, but John fought his way through, using his cane as machete. He kept stopping and breathing in the air. "Something smells wonderful here," he said. He bent down to pick up bits of juniper and hudsonia. A little farther along he plucked up a handful of lichen and poverty grass. He sniffed at it like a wine vintner smelling a cork. "Ah-hah—this is it," he said. I stepped closer and he pressed it to my nose. When I had gotten a good snort, he jammed the whole large clump into his pocket.

We made our way out to the edge of the cliff and again he stared at the ocean, now from a hundred feet above it.

"Beautiful," I said again, and we both laughed.

"I miss the days of the old ocean liners," he said.

Below us the breakers roared and curled over themselves: a plunge, a crash, a kick of spray cut through with sunlight.

"I spent a lot of time up here when I was writing *The Great Beach*," John said. "I rented a cabin for a few weeks. It was like this time, with Kristi in the hospital, in a way. Just me living alone and eating cans of stew. Kristi didn't like it, of course; she felt I was deserting her. But I needed to do it. Beston's wife said of him that he could only write about a landscape if he became a part of it. I needed that too. I didn't want to be just a visitor." He waved his cane over the water and then turned back toward the scruffy landscape of the dune.

"Scientists give names to things," he said. "They label things. They call poverty grass *Hudsonia* and beach grass *Ammophilia* and gold-enrod *Solidago*. They're good with fancy names, but what they never quite get at is the sense that the whole landscape is in movement. Things are always interacting and *moving*. Science can't describe that." He smiled and leaned his head back in the sun.

"I will never forget my trip to Greenland. It was magnificent. I was sent by a magazine for retired doctors, though I wasn't a retired doctor myself, even a doctor of letters. I watched some ice calve off the side of the glacier with a tremendous noise like an explosion. The ice dropped into the water and stunned the fish, and then the gulls swarmed in to feed on the fish. So much movement. One movement leading to another. Interacting. The whole landscape vibrating."

It was past noon. John looked content enough to stay out there all afternoon, staring at the sea, but it was time for him to return home and get ready for his visit to Kristi at the rehab center. We worked our way back up the path, away from the ocean. Soon we were driving back down 6A toward Brewster. We stopped at the grocery store to get John some sourdough bread and cider for lunch. As we were walking down the sidewalk, John accidentally opened the wrong door and stepped into a beauty parlor, then apologized and backed out. "It isn't senility," he explained. "I've always been like that."

I drove him home. As we stood on the front porch saying goodbye, he told me he had had a magnificent day. Then he waved his cane at the railings along his porch. "We'll have to get rid of those soon," he said. "When Kristi comes home in two weeks, we're going to get a ramp put in for a wheelchair. And we'll have to have someone living here round the clock."

Deborah was right. We were coming to the end of something.

I went home and had lunch with Nina and told her about my time with John. After we finished, I decided to jump in the car and return to Coast Guard Beach. The idea of getting out to the point where Henry Beston's house had stood was still stuck in my head, and if I couldn't do it with John, I'd go it alone. By two o'clock, forty minutes later, I was back on the beach, hiking south over the low-tide sand, my backpack stuffed with my telescope, bird books, journals, a copy of *The Outermost House*, and a quart of beer. I walked hard into the wind, thinking of John's weakening condition and by contrast of my own strong legs, reveling in the hike and the spectacle around me. While I'd made it a point in my life to live in beautiful places, I had never lived anywhere quite as wild as Beston's beach. Our house on the edge was wild, true, but this was more extreme. I tried to imagine what it had been like to be alone on this sandbar, eating, drinking, and sleeping to the constant loud roar of the surf, what John had called the plunge and seethe.

I thought of John sniffing the poverty grass and lichen, the tilt of his head as he listened to the sea, the way he had leaned his head back, closed his eyes, and soaked in the sun. Unlike Thoreau's, his appreciation of the natural world had not diminished near the end of his life. But like a lot of older people, John's thoughts had turned to the beyond, though his beyond had no angels playing harps on puffy clouds.

"Do you believe in traditional religion?" I had asked.

"Nature is my religion," he said, almost brusquely. Then, more quietly: "The ceremony of nature."

It seemed to me that this was the point where the thought and work of John Hay and Henry Beston intersected. Not that Beston had necessarily influenced Hay in the usual sense. More that they had both come to similar conclusions, having deeply experienced the natural world.

Beston wrote habitually of the year's ritual, the movement of the sun that still, on the deepest level, leads us through the year. How we involve ourselves with the ritual of the year had also been John Hay's preoccupation. In this sense, animals served as companions—companions with their own complex lives—and as role models for living in tune with the earth's rhythms. Of the swallows in his barn, John wrote: "Theirs is a ceremonial with an earth experience and rhythmic consistency behind it." His effort, especially in later years, had been to live within this consistency, to live within a deeper sense of time. No wonder the punch clock so bothered him; it was an affront to the kind of time he had spent his life trying to become part of.

"A year in outer nature is the accomplishment of a tremendous ritual," wrote Beston. For Beston, and for John, life was elevated when calendars and clocks were replaced by the respiratory rhythm of the ocean and the slow journey of the sun. By immersing themselves, they sank into place, "wedging down," as Thoreau had put it. This was hardly something new, of course. More something old. For the Hopi Indians, for instance, the way of the sun and its movements were the central fact of their lives. Here was a better, older way to be.

From Beston's beach I stared out at the Atlantic: the greens in the troughs of the waves, the blue farther out, the foam spitting up. I listened to the rumbling, "the eternal unquiet of the sea." For two hours I walked, crunching through dried-out crab carcasses and shells, down to the Nauset break and then back along the marsh, which with low tide was no longer an inland sea. Gray clouds now scumbled the sky and blocked the sun, and I realized that John and I had probably seen the better part of the day. I circled around and doubled back to a spot that I imagined was fairly close to where Beston's house had stood. Then I climbed the dune and stared first at the sea and then at the marsh.

I watched birds through my binoculars for a while. An injured black duck slapped out of the water on clown's feet over the mudflats, where it was set upon by a gull. With weather coming in, the duck wouldn't make it through the night. Then I saw two small birds that

I couldn't identify. They were sparrowlike, with yellow faces and black masks, and they picked along the wrack line. I skimmed through the bird books, deciding against horned larks and northern wheateaters as too exotic. After a while I gave up and let the birds go unnamed, which didn't seem to faze them.

By then clouds had completely buried the sun, except for an occasional shaft of light that broke through. I was cold and decided to head home. Forty minutes later I was back below the Coast Guard station. From the beach, the building looked too upright, not wide enough, like an overly proper matron, the roof a funny red hat and the dormers surprisingly pert breasts. Then, just as I was about to climb the path back to the station and my car, the sun came out again, giving the day back its morning warmth. The clouds had been streaming from south to north, and it looked like the rest of the afternoon would be clear, and so the weather's change changed my plans. I doubled back again toward Beston's home site, this time wending my way along the edge of the marsh, for a while following the prints of a red fox. The sun lit up the previously drab beach grass a radiant gold, and purple-blue shadows stretched back toward the ocean. A full tide cycle had turned, and the water was running in along the inlets. It streamed over the glasswort, rippling and shining a deep bold cerulean blue as a northern harrier lifted up above the marsh.

Back at the site of Beston's home, I took up my former spot. I sat huddled in the dune, out of the wind and facing the dying sun, and conducted a little ceremony of my own. I drank the beer I'd brought along, and once the alcohol began bubbling up inside me, I pulled out my copy of Beston's book. No one was around to think I was foolish to be reading out loud to myself. And so, with the setting sun as my audience, I read the book's most celebrated passage:

> My house completed, and tried and not found wanting by a first Cape Cod year, I went there to spend a fortnight in September. The fortnight ending, I lingered on, and as the year lengthened into autumn, the beauty and mystery of this earth and outer sea so possessed and held me that I could not go. The world to-day is sick to its thin blood for lack of elemental things, for fire before the hands, for water welling from the earth, for air, for the dear earth itself underfoot. In my world of beach and dune these elemental presences lived and had their being, and under their arch there moved an incomparable pageant of the year.

My ceremony ended just before the sun dropped over Eastham. I watched the last molten sliver disappear and then decided that by focusing exclusively on the sun, I had been neglecting the ocean. I climbed back over the dune and found that the other side of the world was offering up a mystery of its own. A full moon had risen, white and clean and distinct against the darkening purple sky, perfectly balancing the setting sun on the dune's western side. I didn't pretend to have found any final, profound answers, but for the moment at least, I felt in balance with the world.

I thought again of John standing on the cliff that morning: the way he had looked while staring out at the sea, his long white-silver hair and foggy gaze. If you were of the mind, you might describe the look on his face as "saintly," but I knew John well enough by now to know he was no saint. He had written that terns went about their lives with both "agitation and ceremony," and for all his guru status on Cape Cod, I understood that agitation welled up almost as often as reverence in his chest. But in the end he had come closer to living a life of ceremony than anyone I knew. That was what was important. Echoing Beston, he wrote of the terns: "They seem to me like explorers from a great outer world from which we have been excluding ourselves. The closest I can come to it is going down to the shore again, where I am exposed to stripped-down, elemental demands."

As he'd grown older, John's quest had become increasingly spiritual, and the writing mirrored this, sometimes so ethereal it almost floated off the page. But what kept it anchored was the earth itself, what Beston called "elemental things" and John called "elemental demands." What were these? The smells of the lichen and poverty grass he had jammed under my nose, the feel of the sun burning his face, the seething rumble of the sea. These were the things he couldn't let go of. Wanting to get below "the abstractions we substitute for reality," John had lived close to the root of things. Long ago, in an essay called "The Magnet of Spring," he wrote: "Over the years, I have come to look for the same events to be renewed: the singing of peepers in the bogs, the arrival of alewives in the brook. I want to feel raw life, raw as a codfish pulled out of the cold sea, quiet as an ant, clean running as a swallow, deep throated as a Great Black-backed Gull." That "raw life" was the gift given him, and his words were the gift he gave back: his daily oblation performed within the sanctuary of the studio.

But standing there balanced between setting sun and rising moon, I was not really concerned with John's words. What concerned me was the ceremonial of his days. Yes, he had the usual human worries and troubles, but like the terns, he had made ceremony, not mere achievement, the central focus of his life. The Sioux Indian Gemma Lockhart had called John her "arrow-shooter," the one who had pointed her toward truer goals. I had begun to see him that way, too. If we just paid lip service to loving nature, what was the point? It was John's life, even more than his books, that I admired. He had lived, as best a compromised, modern human being could, close to essentials. He had led an elemental life.

6

In Retreat

I n an early conversation, John told me of the dream he had had when he first came to Cape Cod, of his house, his new house on Dry Hill, floating out on the bay. Fifteen years later he wrote about that dream in *Nature's Year:* "Cape Cod reels out into the Atlantic. I saw our house when it was new as a ship above the trees." Now, after our trip to Coast Guard Beach, I couldn't shake the image of Henry Beston's Outermost House drifting over the flooded marsh, those windows bobbing like eyes.

I don't know what John made of all these floating houses, but I was beginning to have my own ideas. They seemed a sign of impermanence, of the fact that all pastoral adventures are temporary, all golden ages brief. I'm sure my interpretation was influenced by my sense that I would soon be leaving Cape Cod and our house on the edge. I wasn't ready yet for the year to be over, but it was starting to look like I would be offered a job at a university a thousand miles away.

Unlike John, I wouldn't be wedging down into one place for decade after decade. But in my current frame of mind, it seemed that *all* homes had watery foundations, that what we imagined as forever never was. Of course, John's own adventure in retreat had been remarkable in its consistency and duration, putting the lie to the usual fleeting nature of such enterprises. But John's retreat was temporary as well, even if it was a longer sort of temporary. And though he didn't know it yet, his journey on Dry Hill was almost over.

One night in late March Deborah Diamond gave me a call. "I hope I'm not intruding," she said. "But it would be great if you could take John out for a walk. I think he needs a guy friend."

At first I laughed at the idea, but she went on to explain the new situation on Dry Hill. Since Kristi had come home from the hospital, the Hays had had nurses around the clock at their house. After sixty years of independence, they were now living as dependents, and this did not sit well with John. Space was his cherished value, and now the space of his home had been invaded. One of the nurses had driven up to the house in a giant SUV with a huge American flag draped over the rear window. "You write books and stuff, don't you?" the woman asked when she met John.

When I called, John seemed relieved to hear from me. "Just to see the shore would bring me some sanity," he said. "To get outside into the world."

He suggested I come between two and three, but at two on the dot my phone rang. "Dave?" he said. "I'm ready to go."

I threw my binoculars and bird books in the car and drove over to Dry Hill. John was standing outside when I arrived. He looked terribly thin, and the binoculars hanging from his neck seemed like a weight pulling him toward the ground.

"Thank God you're here," he said. "I've been surrounded by women."

He said *women* in a way that made you half expect he'd follow it with *folk*. Though he was hardly a chauvinist, and though women —from Gemma Lockhart to Deborah Diamond to Janice Riley, who was making a film about his book *The Run*—were some of his dearest friends, he was old-fashioned enough for the word *womenfolk* not to have seemed entirely out of place.

John often did seem from another time. There were no answering machines to pick up when you called Dry Hill, and there sure as hell were no computers or cell phones. I noticed the tennis shirt he wore beneath his coat and thought of a story that the writer Jennifer Ackerman told me. Jennifer had organized an anthology of nature writing and asked John to write the preface. When the book came out, she had sent all the contributors, including John, T-shirts as a thank-you. Before mailing John's shirt, she had called Dry Hill and asked him what size he would like. There was a long pause before he replied. "I don't know exactly," he said. "I've never worn a T-shirt before."

As we shook hands hello, I noticed that John's hair was even longer than it had been, flowing down his neck in thin, almost silvery white waves. He explained that before we drove off on our adventure we had some work to do: we needed to get Deuce, the schnauzer, back into his cage. This took a little doing, and I thought again how strange it was for the Hays to have become recent owners of a peppy little dog.

"I'm sorry, Deuce," John said as we finally coaxed the dog into the cage. "But if we let you free, you'll crap the rug."

Once we were back outside, John pointed at the early blooming all around the property. A cherry tree right in front of the house was exploding with deep maroon. This led to talk of the early spring and, naturally, of the strangely warm weather. As we drove down the driveway, I mentioned that I'd just read that a slice of Antarctic ice the size of Rhode Island had calved off into the sea.

"The only ones who don't believe the world is warming are the politicians in power," John said. "Good god. Don't they ever walk outside? These people don't believe in cause and effect."

He looked ready to launch into a longer political diatribe, but then reined himself in and smiled. "Let's check if there are fish yet," he said.

We got in the car and drove over to Stony Brook. The day before it had rained heavily, and the brook was pouring downstream in great silver surges. The just-budding green of the briers was highlighted with blood red, and insects rose up from the water like silver flashes at the edge of vision.

"Do you see any?" John asked me as we neared the water.

I peered into the copper-colored stream. I counted six herring in one of the larger middle pools. In the sunlight they looked violet-backed and almost transparent. "A half-dozen or so," I said.

118

"Just scouts," he said.

I mentioned the violet color.

"Another metamorphosis. You know, they actually change color as they swim upstream. Let's see a human do that!"

I asked him when the peak of the run was.

"It really gets going in mid-April," he said. "Around tax day. Then the stream is choked with fish."

The few herring in the brook now were circling, recovering from throwing themselves up the last tiny waterfall while gathering energy for the next. In *The Run*, John had written: "I found that they had a circling motion as they moved upstream, within the greater circle of coming in from deep water and returning after they spawned, which was characteristic of other schooling fishes, as well as flocks of birds, not to mention the circle of the seasons within the year, and by collective inference, the lives of men."

"I'm not the linear type," John said once in an interview. "I circle like alewives and terns and herring gulls. I think it's more interesting to be circular. You go farther. You take in more."

There were two other clusters of people at the run, and soon one of the clusters migrated toward John. This was his home turf, after all, and a member of the group came up and asked for his autograph. "He's the most famous herring person," someone else said. John scrawled down his name on a scrap of paper and dispensed tidbits about the run. A few people gathered around him while I wandered off.

When I returned, we walked up to the spot where the brook poured out of the pond. As we crossed the road, I noticed that John almost tripped twice, recovering both times with little hops and jogs. He was much weaker than he had been in the fall, and as usual I wanted to reach out and grab his arm but held myself back. After a short while we reached the last gushing waterfall, the herring's final hurdle before they shot into the relative quiet of the pond. Nina, watching the fish achieve their final goal, had said of the pond, "This is herring heaven." However, today no fish were making the final ascent, and after studying the water for a while, we went back to the car.

Earlier in March, Nina and I had taken a trip to Belize. As with most places I traveled to, both actual and metaphoric, John Hay had been there first. In fact, our friend and tour guide, Alan Poole, who took us out to a small biological station called Wee Wee Caye, had given John a similar tour a decade before.

One afternoon we took a trip in the whaler to snorkel around a caye farther south. As we passed a small uninhabited island, Alan explained that it was the home of the southernmost osprey nest in the hemisphere. The bird rose up as if on cue, its shining white head much lighter than those of its northern cousins. I remembered something John had written: "The osprey is a power of its own, sacred to a million years. More men are needed who in thinking well of an osprey do not thereby think better of themselves."

Later that evening, back on Wee Wee Caye, I watched the frigate birds that John had first told me about back on our Cape Cod marsh. They floated over the small island on their long batlike wings, like kites pointed into the Caribbean wind. I had to agree with the birds' official upgrading to "magnificent."

At night we took our mattresses out to the dock and stared up through binoculars at a sky unpolluted by light. With the added magnification, every speck of the sky was crammed with white dots, a massive spray of stars.

"When he was here, John watched the stars through my binocs, and you know what he said?" Alan asked me.

I shook my head.

"He said, 'They look like fish eggs.'"

On the drive home I brought up my visit to Belize. John mentioned his own trip there, as well as his trip to Costa Rica, during which he had met the renowned ornithologist Alexander Skutch. "I was amazed that he had no screens in his cabin. He let the birds fly through the house and eat the insects. He had birds perching on his finger. He seemed to have entered into their world, rather than just studying it."

I had read some of Skutch's work, as well as criticisms of it. "He's been accused of anthropomorphizing too much for a scientist," I said.

"Who don't they crucify for that?" he said. "Anyone with feeling. Petty technocrats. They tar us all with that brush. They love facts and loathe the unseen."

I said that I knew from personal experience that scientists often seemed irked by the willingness of mere naturalists or, worse, generalists to make broad statements about the world. Anyone who wrote in the "nature" genre had experienced what Barry Lopez called "the condescension of some scientists who thought the naturalist not rigorous, not analytic, not detached enough."

"It isn't anthropomorphizing the birds," John said. "It's granting them their own consciousness. I only sort of figured this out later on. Everything was taught to me in the abstract back in school. I had to lose that and learn science. I was taught to believe in so-called objective things enshrined by science, but then I found out that science doesn't know all that much. Science gives us the illusion of control, the idea that we are the great measurers of things. But the trouble with science is that it requires an observer—someone outside—and that affects our entire attitude. It separates us, makes us forget we are part of things. There is a place where science drops off and then something else has to take over. That is the spot where we must make some very unscientific leaps."

John added that he admired the old-time naturalists like E. H. Forbush much more than "all these modern antlike scientists with their dead souls."

Again he was ready to launch into a full diatribe, but then the urge seemed to fade and he fell quiet. He had changed dramatically in the past months, and his energy could suddenly desert him. As we drove over to my neighborhood, he stared out the window without speaking. We parked at the landing by the bluff and climbed out of the car. I pointed my telescope at the four or five harbor seals that slumped on Tautog Rock, but John was more interested in the flock of common eiders.

"I sometimes feel like a fog has fallen over me," he said. "I don't know why, but the only thing I seem to care about these days is shore-birds. They make me feel alive again."

We drove back to his house in silence, until we got about halfway up his driveway. Then, using the butt of his cane, John pointed at a small path that squiggled off the road into a decline in the woods.

"That's Berry's Hole down there," he said. "You should walk in before you leave. I was there yesterday. The frogs are starting to sing. The place is alive."

After dropping him off, I followed his advice. On the way back down the driveway, I pulled over and descended the path. As I half hiked and half slid, all I could think of was how steep, bumpy, and brier-filled the hill was. I wondered how the hell John had made it down and back; the acorns alone should have sent him sprawling. But when I reached the little waterhole, I saw that the risk would have been worth it. The vernal pool was covered in shadows, but the shade was lit up by a frog symphony. Occasionally I heard the simple banjo ping of the tree frogs, but the pings were drowned out by the great throb of the peepers. All the nearby land sloped down to the water, and the song of the little frogs echoed and vibrated, washing over me. As quietly as I could, I snuck even closer to the water, to be in the midst of the noise without disturbing the singers. As I sat there, I thought how *peep* was an entirely inadequate word for this deafening roar of spring. I let the noise cover me. The pulsing song was a declaration of the season—a wild, excessive yodel.

As the spring days lengthened, my visits to John's house became much less formal and more relaxed. Time is an underrated element in the growth of friendships, and now I would sometimes stop in to see if John and Kristi needed anything, or just to say hello. Knowing John, being friends with John, added a deeper layer to my last days on Cape Cod. A sense of great privilege and gratitude came with his friendship. It was, I told Nina, like being able to drive down the street to Walden to chat with Thoreau.

At the same time, although I had abandoned my biography, I still felt the urge to preserve my meetings with John. But I had some trepidation about turning my encounters with him into sentences and paragraphs. I wasn't ready to start writing, which would mean thinking about John in the past tense. Studying anything, be it tern or osprey or heron or human, changes the interaction itself, and chronicling those interactions alters them even more. Purity is lost for the sake of permanence.

In the meantime, Deborah Diamond and I both noticed John slowing down even more. More than once I had imagined John's end as a final collapsing into the ground, similar to his lying down on the marsh back in December. "My body begins its long shudder into humus," Wendell Berry had written. And that, of course, was how it would be for John: after a lifetime of writing about natural circles and cycles, he would feed the earth and start the circle again.

John's actual life, however, didn't always stick to the script of quiet acceptance. The problem was that he was a human being. In watching my father die of cancer, I had come to believe that the art of dying well was as vital as the art of living, and the art of dying was one of relinquishment. Now I was hoping to observe and learn from the way John faced the end of his life. Ideally, I would have liked to write of how a lifetime of studying the seasons allowed him to accept the end, how he would sink peacefully into the ground. The problem was that this wasn't always true. John was, to a certain extent, accepting of what was happening. "Our inability to give things up is part of an overall acquisitiveness," he had said to me at Paine's Creek. "Life is just another thing we clutch to." But he had less philosophic and lofty moments. In fact, he sometimes sounded pissed off. He loved his wild life. He didn't want it to end. He didn't want to die. "Age is no damn good," he'd said during an earlier visit. And recently, "I can barely make it down the damn driveway." Still, he wouldn't simply let go of walking. "I'd rather die than give that up," he said.

In other ways, too, he was raging against the dying of the light, going down kicking, though that wasn't it exactly either. It wasn't death that seemed to scare and frustrate him so much as not being able to encounter the world. His fading vision, for instance, was particularly painful. Unfortunately, on the way to his final leaving, other things were left strewn along the roadside. Haltingly, he was being forced to abandon his daily work as well as his independence and solitude.

One of the things John was raging against was the fact that he was no longer in control of the story of his life. Suddenly to have all these other people—nurses and caretakers, not to mention me—crowding his house meant giving up autonomy. Worse still, he had now finished the book he had been working on, and he wondered if he would be able to produce another. It was as if he were wrestling to keep control, not just of his life but of his voice.

In *The Environmental Imagination*, Lawrence Buell noted that the archetypal plot of much of nature writing is one of relinquishment, the evolving understanding that life is not so much about the getting of things as the ability to let things go, just as Thoreau let go and simplified when he retreated to Walden. For John, coming to Dry Hill had been a process of leaving behind what the world valued. Here he had discovered both what he valued and what he had to give away.

Now, in this time of great relinquishing, he had already arranged to give away his greatest possession (though he would never use that word to describe it). When he died, Dry Hill would become common ground, returned to the community, never to be developed. In April I talked to Mark Robinson, of the Compact of Cape Cod Conservation Trusts, and he told me how John had ceded his property to the town as conservation land. The only exception was an acre or two near the top of Dry Hill that had been put aside for his son, Charlie, to build on if he chose. Otherwise, all fifty-plus acres would remain as a small island of undeveloped wildness.

But it wasn't only things, or even land, that John was in the process of letting go of. Buell writes that "the more radical relinquishment is to give up individual autonomy itself, to forgo the illusion of mental and even bodily apartness from one's environment." John had spent his life testing the permeable boundaries of self, trying to see where he ended and a tern began. His efforts to leave himself behind, to fly out of himself into other creatures, had always required letting go of things we all naturally hold hard to. To jump out of self, to leave self and identity behind, required a trust that you could return to what was abandoned, though the self you did return to might be permanently changed.

I thought again of Fools Crow, the Lakota Sioux elder whom John had visited in South Dakota. John wrote: "The plainness of the small room in which the old man sat was a testimony to his character. It was empty of possession, and of any need to possess. As a wise advisor and healer to his people, Fools Crow had been given many presents, but he gave them all away."

One day I asked John about this.

"What Gemma told me was that in her mother's culture, if you like something enough, you should give it away. That makes it precious in a way it wouldn't otherwise be."

Like Fools Crow, John now was "a grave old man," with a "look of unshakeable dignity and faith."

Though I often tried, there was really no way for me to truly empathize with the diminishment of old age and the finality of what John was facing. I was now about the age that John had been when he had begun to publish his books, and my sense of the time ahead of me was still relatively limitless. I was not there yet and didn't understand the place he had come to—as usual, he had gotten there first. And John, for his part, could never return to the energy and power that I still took for granted.

During those last weeks on Cape Cod, I often thought of a story that Bob Finch had told me about a summer he spent working in John Hay's studio. At the time Bob was a struggling young writer, and John, in a characteristically generous manner, had offered him a small plot of land at the foot of Dry Hill. Though Bob had some trepidation at working in the shadow of his master, he of course accepted this offer. It was around this time, in the early 1970s, that the Cape Cod summers—the clogged traffic on Route 6A, the constant noise, the tourists in the stores—became too much for John, and he set out on another search for space. He found that space in the little town of Bremen, Maine, where he bought a home on the water, and he and Kristi migrated there during the summer season.

During one of those first summers, Bob, who was busy building his home at the foot of Dry Hill, had nowhere to write. John offered him the use of his studio while he was away, and Bob took him up on it. If it felt a little strange to be living in the shadow of the master, how did it feel to work at his actual desk?

"The thing was, he didn't put anything away," Bob said. "It was as if he'd left in the middle of a sentence. I tried to respect his privacy, but there were open pages and manuscripts just staring up at me."

One of the things staring up at him was a passage about the feeling of abandonment, the sense of being lost and alone, that comes with old age. John wasn't yet sixty, but time was already streaming past. Life was short. The sentence that caught Bob's eye was this one: "Hold on, hold on, *help is not coming.*" Bob was struck by the line in part because John rarely wrote anything so baldly personal.

Bob forgot about the sentence until some years later. Then, while reading one of John's books, he came upon it again. It was the same sentence—"Hold on, hold on, help is not coming"—with one crucial difference. This time the sentiments of being lost were put into a description of stranded whales.

I had known that we would move out of the edge house for the summer; after all, that was part of our deal. But now I learned that it would be more than just the end of our time there. The owners called to say they had sold the house and to inform us that we would have to move out by early June. Our idyll by the sea was coming to an abrupt end.

I was surprised. The family who rented the place to us had owned it for over forty years. But of course it was the way things had been going over the past few years on Cape Cod. Everyone was cashing in, and the few places with character that were left were being torn down. Nina and I had harbored secret dreams of one day buying the property, but these were, of course, unrealistic. Bought in 1960 for $15,500, it now sold for millions.

That startling phone call was followed by another. I was officially offered a job as a professor at a university in the South. Nina and I had discussed our desire to start a family and our inability to support ourselves with our writing alone. We did not have the resources of John Hay, and Cape Cod was a land of high real estate prices and few jobs.

I put off the decision but knew that our time on the Cape was growing short. John had written extensively about the need for human beings to marry the land they love, to commit to it and form a deeper relationship, and I had taken his words seriously. But while I believed in those words, I was of a different generation, a different time. Maybe it wasn't possible simply to repeat and relive the old verities. The world was more crowded, land more expensive. "Marriage to a place is something we need to realize in our culture, but not all of us are the marrying kind," John Daniel wrote.

I believed I was the marrying kind, but my attempts to wed myself to Cape Cod had met with constant frustration. With increasing desperation we had tried to buy a home, but now the median price had shot up to over $370,000. Sometimes I felt as if I were in some sort of bad dream: as I ran toward the homes we tried to buy, they kept receding beyond our grasp. I understood that my personal troubles were no great tragedy, but I did believe that my story was indicative of a larger economic drama. Nina and I had pushed our way into the middle class, and if we couldn't afford to live on Cape Cod, then it stood to reason that others in our situation couldn't either. Now we were contemplating joining the migration off-Cape.

That leaving was the logical thing to do didn't make it any less painful. It occurred to me that our time near the water was as close as I would ever get to living my own Walden. As spring poured in, there were days when an almost manic energy, a crazed enlivening, spilled over into me as I walked out to the swirling world of the bluff. I loved that strip of sand and rock, and even the row of million-dollar houses couldn't change the wildness of the place once the winds ripped over the water. And that wildness in turn spoke to something wild in me, until my whole body hummed like a tuning fork.

We knew that leaving the edge house meant leaving a happy and productive period of our lives. More than that, we had a sneaking suspicion that we were leaving the best place we had ever lived and the best place we would ever live. We'd be losing something when we left, something subtler than a nice view. We were going to miss the raw stimulation of living so close to the water and the bluff. And we were going to miss a deeper connection that we couldn't yet put into words.

John, too, was facing a time of deep transition.

Over on Dry Hill, chaos reigned. Kristi went back into the hospital, then returned home again. The round-the-clock care would now be permanent, and John seemed further weakened by all the commotion and the people. One day when Deborah was visiting, John handed her a book of Yeats poems and asked her to read "Sailing to Byzantium":

This is no country for old men. The young
In one another's arms, birds in trees,
—Those dying generations—at their song,
The salmon-falls, the mackerel-crowded seas,
Fish, flesh, or fowl, commend all summer long

Whatever is begotten, born, and dies.
Caught in that sensual music all neglect
Monuments of unageing intellect.

An aged man is but a paltry thing,
A tattered coat upon a stick, unless
Soul clap its hands and sing, and louder sing
For every tatter in its mortal dress
Nor is there singing school but studying
Monuments of its own magnificence;
And therefore I have sailed the seas and come
To the holy city of Byzantium.

Deborah continued, reading the last two verses, while John leaned back in his chair and closed his eyes. When she was done, there was silence in the studio. Then, after a few minutes, he asked her to read it again. When she had read the last line of the poem—*Of what is past, or passing, or to come*—for the second time, he stood up abruptly and walked to the door. He opened it and glanced back at Deborah. He had a solemn look on his face, as if he were about to make a grave pronouncement. "Now you think that over while I take a leak," he said, breaking into his little-boy smile.

The next day I visited Deborah at the museum. We stood, as usual, on opposite sides of the library desk.

"Lately there are times when I'm with John and it feels like he isn't there," she said. "But then there's a day like yesterday when he's back—when he's awake and alive. Then it's like being with a perfect sentence."

I said I knew exactly how she felt.

"So many people lead dead lives," she said. "He's at the end of things, but so many people near the end are not even aware. He's at the end of things, but he's still close to life." This thought excited her and she raised her voice to try to share the feeling. "And he's still here! I left there yesterday in a great mood—just that John's still here and it's finally spring. Sometimes I think about him in the past, but then suddenly, yesterday, he was back in the present again! We were working, trying to transcribe an old journal, and he kept saying, 'I wonder if there are fish at the brook?' Finally I closed my notebook and said, 'You don't want to work, do you?' So we played hooky and drove over to Stony Brook to check on the herring. He still cares so much about those damn fish!"

She went to get a piece of paper and handed it to me. "We cleaned out his notebooks yesterday. He wanted to toss everything. This was just one of the scraps he told me to throw out. He didn't have any idea what year he wrote it, sometime in the late fifties probably. None of his notes have dates."

I started to laugh as I read.

"He also types terribly," she added.

He did type terribly. I remembered that his studio had a note on the wall from his editor after John had sent her a manuscript that his daughter-in-law had typed for him. "From the well-typed manuscript I was at first worried that someone else was claiming to be you," the editor had written, "but no one can write like John Hay."

Now I tried to decipher John's note: "STny brook valley—I am seized by that tremencous fudckuty ti breeding and buryh that keeps the planet on course in spite of us."

Despite the poor typing, I didn't need a translation. It was spring, after all, and I too had been seized by that tremendous fecundity. The sights and sounds of the past weeks were overwhelming: the mergansers and song sparrows and spring peepers, the foxes and exuberant seals; and I thought that as usual, John had it right. Spring was surging, and the planet was—despite us, despite everything—on course.

7

THE SOURCE

My year by the sea was winding down, but spring brought with it more than its usual resurgence. John felt a temporary lifting and asked me if I would drive him over to the herring run to see the returning fish.

It was a spectacular spring day when we visited, and the herring were running hard. We sat on a bench and watched the fish and the people watching the fish. The return of the herring was one of the annual migrations that had deepened John's life. It was part of his ceremony, one of the great events that marked the turning of the year.

He wasn't alone in this. For thousands of years the native Wampanoags looked to the herring's return as a heartening sign of spring, not to mention as a form of protein. Later the Pilgrims wrote about how the herring runs saved them after their first hard winters. Such an abundance after long absence. And the sheer reliability of it! Thousands and thousands of fish coming back—fish you could scoop up in baskets—every spring, for as long as men could remember.

"These fish were held in high estimation by our fathers and their annual appearance was ever welcomed," Josiah Paine wrote of the herring, also known as alewives, in the 1700s. By 1787, Brewster had claimed sections of the river and appointed an alewife committee, a practice that has continued to the present day. By the 1800s the creek was called Mill River, but it has had many other names, including Sauquatuckett, Herring River, and Sautuckett. The historian Paul Schneider wrote: "West Brewster became known as Factory Village for the five mills along the banks of the never-mighty Stony Brook." But still the town fought to build side canals to give the herring their right of way, knowing how much the fish provided.

The section of the stream that John and I watched was at the headwaters of Stony Brook, right below Mill Pond. The fresh water of Stony Book mingles with the incoming salt water until it transforms itself into the wholly saltwater Paine's Creek, which empties into Cape Cod Bay. Where we sat, the brook was chopped up by fish ladders, dams, and waterfalls, through which the herring maneuvered as they made their way back to lower Mill Pond. The herring fought against the current, throwing themselves up and over the falls in preposterous arcs "like miniature salmon" as John said.

After sitting quietly for a while, I asked John about the first year he spent studying the herring. I was interested for many reasons, not least because the herring had led to his first true breakthrough as a writer. John thought about it before answering.

"The herring were a revelation," he said finally. "It's so easy for an artist just to turn permanently inward. The herring forced me to learn about other lives, to get outside of myself. They were also a kind of entry into the ocean. I walked all the way down to the ocean along Stony Brook. I'd go barefoot and get the feel of the place. The whole hill was bare—all the vegetation has come up since then. So you felt it and could see it. I watched the herring come in in a sort of military fashion. Once I saw them come in at night, flickers of silver in the black. And this is when I first found out that everything is metamorphosing all the time. That the world is full of transformations."

He paused for a second and let his head drop toward the ground. But then he lifted it again, like a driver who has caught himself dozing. He smiled to himself at the memory of that first curiosity and epiphany.

"And it turned out that those fish connected me to the community. I ended up getting involved with starting the Natural History Museum because someone heard I was writing a book about the herring. People around town caught wind of what I was doing. A woman I knew in Harwich said one day, 'I hear you're writing a book about the sex life of fish.' 'That's a reasonable way to put it,' I said to her. That's what it's all about, after all.

" 'Oh, they're just a bunch of fish,' people would say. 'What's interesting about fish?' My favorite aunt, Alice, told me I'd picked the most boring subject in the world. But as I read more of the natural science about fish, I began to think that the herring had tremendous stamina. The fact of the matter is that they come in as saltwater fish and the fresh water is a great strain on their system. They swim in the deeper, colder temperatures during the wintertime, but then it begins to heat up and they come in here and they have a special adaptation to their kidneys. They don't want to stay any longer than they have to, because like us, they're afraid of strange new environments. To go between two different environments, one salt and one fresh, takes some guts. Not guts the way we think of it. Guts and kidneys."

He laughed, and then fell quiet. After a few minutes I asked him what Conrad Aiken had thought of his book about the herring, *The Run.*

"Conrad liked it quite a lot," he said. "Almost too much. He said to me, 'Now you've done it. You'll never do anything better.'" John shook his head at the memory. "He believed authors go on repeating themselves when they get to a certain level. He said, 'After this one you'll never write anything again.' I said, 'What the hell are you talking about?' He said people have a tendency to keep writing like themselves forever and ever." He shook his head again. "I thought, 'Oh god, my life has come to an end.' I was very upset by that. I said to him, 'Well, I suppose I better throw in the towel then.'"

Back at home I dug into my pile of books and articles and photos. While I had abandoned my biography of John, I still felt some of the biographer's pleasure in unearthing the secrets of his life. It seemed to me that Stony Brook was the center of his mystery. The fish weren't the only creatures that experienced a transformation as they worked their way upstream. It had also been the place where an uncertain young man had become the confident elder I now knew. It only heightened my interest that John had been almost exactly my age when that transformation occurred.

It was in early April 1955 that the herring changed his life. By then John was almost forty and had suffered through a long period of acute doubt and uncertainty. "Anxiety seized me and held on for a long time," he wrote. Almost a decade had passed since he had moved to Cape Cod to learn at Conrad Aiken's knee, and he had accomplished surprisingly little, at least by the world's standards. He had published one slight book of poems, which hardly sold and which, while getting a few decent reviews, spoke in a voice not yet his own, a voice that echoed with lyric remnants of another century, sentences left over from his schooling. That book was followed by a travel narrative about finding America (written well before Jack Kerouac's was published) called "Looking for My Country," a manuscript he finally abandoned. All the while, famous Conrad was right down the street, churning out books in factory mode. In contrast, John's words dribbled out.

Maybe in his worst moments he felt something like panic, comparing his ever-increasing age to the ages when other writers had published their first books. Did it occur to him that he was closing in on the age Aiken had been when they had first met, and that Aiken was already an established literary icon then? John had two young children and another on the way, and he had done little writing outside of freelance articles and reviews. "I wasn't confident as a writer," he told the *Boston Globe* forty years later. "I really thought I might have to give up and take a 'real job.' "

Of course, things were not altogether grim. As well as being a period of doubt, the years after he moved to the Cape had been a time of excitement. He'd built a home in the wilderness, after all, and was raising a family with his beautiful young wife. Together they had begun to help create the Museum of Natural History down the road. And John was slowly getting to know his neighbors, too. Along with Nate Black, who cut John's hair for fifty cents, there was Bill Perry, who kept pigeons just as John had done as a child in New Hampshire, and Geneva Cash, who had been imported from the Azores to pick cranberries, and Clint Eldridge, who trapped otters down in the marsh. There were still subsistence farmers left then, people who knew the land they lived on.

But more than anything else there was the place itself. Over the years it had continued to reveal itself as so much more than "a dump" or "a worthless woodlot." It grew on John in an almost literal sense, day by day, by accretion, just as the stumpy oaks grew until they blocked his once clear view of the bay. "Here at least was a place where life was new again, and open to the unknown," he wrote. When did he start to understand that in this landscape he'd found his geographical match, or at least the perfect place for mind to mimic land? He had majored in English literature at Harvard and had no training in the sciences. But his real study, he began to discover, almost against his will, was phenology, the discipline of watching phenomena change as the seasons turned. Didn't anyone else notice how perfectly the natural world seemed to work? Didn't anyone else thrill to its exquisite timing? He listened as the peepers announced spring with their deafening symphony, vibrating the ponds and marshes. He walked down the hill to Berry's Hole, shaped like an "amphitheater for tragic or comic plays and timeless ceremony," and there he heard the tiny frogs singing with the "voices of resurrection." He watched as the swallows returned each spring, carving up the sky, carrying the season in on their backs, and noted how all of life seemed to circle its way through the seasons.

And then there was all the color. The way that in the course of a year the marsh could sprout green, grow vibrant, then sag and burnish to a blazing red-orange. Or the way the cranberry bog shone before harvest and the yellowing beach grass bent and swayed as if urged on by an invisible conductor. Having been raised in New York and being an ambitious young writer, John, like Aiken, must have continued to doubt his choice of a home so far from the center of the literary world. But at other times his choice must have seemed brilliantly inspired. He began to suspect that this place, not New York or Paris, was the center, the thick of it, at least for him. This was where the action was.

If John could be described as a visionary, it was in these years that the vision formed. He may not have written much yet, but as well as learning to write, he was learning the subtle lessons of the seasons. Like Thoreau, he found that watching the year go round was his job. "It was exhilarating to exist on this magic new level," he wrote. He noted secret seasons within the seasons. For instance, he came to understand that there was a time in late summer that resembled a second spring—a time when the bay seemed to spill over with life, the bluefish thrashing and slapping their tails, blind in the frenzy of their boil, sending hundreds of small fish leaping from the water in a fountain of silver. In his journals he recorded being caught up in the spectacle, as clouds of terns wheeled and darted above the thrashing fish. Watching them, he felt the tension of their hovering before they dove, pulling back their wings as they hit the water, then rising up and gobbling down the fish. Gulls hunted too, though less artistically, and prehistoric-looking cormorants dove deep, cutting off the fish's only escape route. All united in gluttony, a great spectacle of fattening.

Staying in one place lent him a surprising perspective on the seasons. "I slowly began to move toward a wider realm," he wrote. Years of watching the world turn taught him a little about what to expect of nature and when to expect it, but at some moments, like summer's second spring, almost too much was going on to keep track of. He scribbled it all down in the hundreds of little notebooks that began to litter his studio. That "tremendous fecundity" seized him.

But with so much going on, so much exuberant life, how to capture it? How to cram all that was happening inside the pages of a book? Novels wouldn't quite work, and his poems weren't sturdy enough to contain it all. On one level the challenge was one of organization. If artists were meant to create worlds, then how was he to create a world that spilled over with change and diversity in the manner of the green world he watched and lived inside? How could he show these miraculous changes without flying out in every direction? How could he capture the sense of movement and seasonal change, of phenomena bursting and dying? How could he communicate the sheer excitement of it? He brooded on this for years and experienced many false starts.

The fish gave him his answer. Amazing how it all came clear in that cold-blooded creature. One fish fighting its way upstream to spawn. John stood among the briers on the shore of Stony Brook during the cold early April of 1955 and watched it squiggle and circle and leap its way back up to the lake where it had hatched. This single fish was a scout, a forerunner of its fellows, most of whom would return later. It was not a startling or novel sight by any means, and perhaps that was part of why it was so perfectly apt. Herring are only ten or twelve inches long, and so common in these parts that townspeople once shoveled them out of the brook with pitchforks. On the one hand they were so plain, but on the other so miraculous. They are anadromous fish that contain adaptations to allow them to live in salt water and then return to breed in fresh, and that battle relentlessly back to their home, their parent stream, up small waterfalls with leaps and thrusts.

And yet even if the fish were spectacular—in both persistence and navigation—it was more than that that made them the perfect subject. More important than the fish themselves was the timing they represented, the way that they, like terns and swallows and peepers, carried in the season. "These fish are tedious," a tourist said to John one day when he was studying the herring. "All they do is repeat the same thing year after year." John laughed. *That was just it!* "The mystery about the travels of birds, eels, monarch butterflies, or alewives is not only a matter of routes or seasonal behavior," he wrote. "It has to do with an internal response to the spinning globe and its unending creative energies. As a result of a respectful regard for other animals we may find that we are being led onto traveled ways that were once invisible to us, and in their deep alliance with natural forces we find a new depth in ourselves."

What particularly fascinated him was the way the fish circled, not just as they rested while advancing upstream but through the year, returning from salt water to fresh and then back to salt. There was something not just circular but symphonic about how it all fit together, and something ineffable. In his notebooks he grappled with trying to put the whole of it into words: "Fish yielding supple currents, beginning and curving—birds in the air lifting, falling, turning. Free circular aspiration. Coordinated layers of leaves, grasses bending in the wind —bush, switch grass, water, rounded stone. Wrong directions—the unexpected. Fish feeling circular dimensions in the waves, motion— seashell, the shape of an egg, the wave of your hand, the curve of your lips, eyes. All in conformity with the curvature of the earth."

Everything about the herring seemed both startling in itself and representative of larger life. "I began to see them, in their crowded, elementary forms, big eyes always staring ahead, as forerunners of all the powers of the seasons," John wrote. "I stood on the banks observing that unswerving passion of theirs obeying some inner need I could not try to name." Telling the story of the fish would be a way to capture all the world's multifarious phenomena in one animal, a way to communicate some of the excitement that had taken hold of him since moving here, and finally a way to spread the news of what he had learned. Both to follow the fish around through the season and to show how the season was opening up inside him.

Another thing that was perfect about the herring as subject was Harry Alexander, the alewife warden, who taught him about these fish. Harry was the old-time pipe-smoking Cape Codder who was chairman of the alewife committee. He spoke with a true Cape Cod accent "that carried echoes of seacoast Britain centuries before," and his rambling stories about the fish were half long-learned truths and half fancy. He watched over the run to make sure that no individual took too many "herrin'," and he did this with such authority that the people of Brewster called him "the King of the Herring Run" or, more simply, "Herrin' Harry." John admired Harry's healthy disrespect for science and found his stories delightful. Through Harry, John believed he could stretch back in time to a former Cape Cod, when locals could sense the tide without even glancing at the water.

How odd, though, that an ambitious young writer from Harvard who had studied Yeats and Keats would settle on herring as a subject, with Herrin' Harry as his guide. Doubts swarmed in immediately, and he joked in his letters about alewives being his muse. John had never been a scientist; who was he to write the herring's story? And if he did, who would read a book about fish? How would this be different from his last unpublished manuscript? If anything, its subject was blander and more obscure, less appealing to readers.

This time, however, excitement overpowered doubt. If his life had been a tug of war between wildness and propriety, then for this one moment, at least, wildness would win out. He threw himself outward, into the world, as vigorously and exuberantly as the herring threw themselves upstream. "This book mirrors an attempt to go farther afield, from one man's center," he wrote in the introductory pages. "Its writing represented a kind of migration in itself." In so many ways the herring worked, both as the thing itself and as metaphor, especially in their struggle to find home. In his abandoned travel book, John had tried to show the need for locality through its obverse, a young man traveling aimlessly through a country where local distinctions were often dying out. Here he could embrace what he called in his notes a "broader definition of home" while singing the seasons of his new home. Of that single fish fighting its way up its parent stream he wrote: "This one seemed to determine the year's direction."

It was a lot to see in a common fish, and it took eyes that had been slowly trained over the years—years when they didn't quite know what they were being trained for. And while this might be hyperbolic, John Hay may have glimpsed one last thing in that lucid moment of vision. He may have seen in the herring's black eyes and shining scales something close to personal salvation, both as man and as writer. He knew that he had found his subject: his first subject, his best subject, in some ways his only subject.

Of course, the transcendent moment is one thing, the work another. There was still the small matter of putting all that he felt onto the page. Over the next year he tried fitfully to describe what he'd seen and what it meant. His first attempts were halting and unsure, at times reading like a book report on fish. He mailed an early draft to Edward

Darling, who would eventually become his editor. Darling wrote back, claiming that the subject was dull: "For God's sake brighten this stuff up. It's quite boring."

In return John sent off a letter that attempted to articulate his vision for the book. Darling replied almost immediately, on May 31, 1956: "I know better now what it is you are trying to do; and I must say your letter of May 26 gets closer to the inside of the subject than anything I've seen from your pen." Perhaps Darling's words provided the necessary encouragement, and perhaps they also suggested a more direct approach to the subject. Whatever the case, somewhere between those early and later drafts something clicked, and the tentative John Hay began to sound more like the visionary he would become. The book transformed from a kind of research project into something new: a complete immersion in the natural world. At the same time the language changed. It opened up, verbs and gerunds starting to fly, sentences mimicking spring's rushed openings, describing not only the fish but the singing peepers and bursting buds. Reading the pages now, one has the sense of something coming alive, of something long frozen thawing. John's words woke, and, caught up in that waking, he began to take more risks.

"The temperatures edged toward the fifties," he wrote, "and there were deep new meetings between the moles and the worms." Now John had found a way to communicate the minutes from those meetings. His doubts were not behind him, of course, but for the moment they had been overrun. He was on to it, and he spent hours typing in the studio.

When *The Run* appeared five years later, it was immediately regarded as what it was: a work obviously original and inspired. *Silent Spring* was yet to be published, and Aldo Leopold had been one of the few to sound a similar note since Thoreau's time. Henry Beston could have been seen as a progenitor, particularly in the excited communication of seasonal change, but John's approach was something different altogether, a message from *inside*. The reviews were universally strong, and the book eventually won its author prizes and acclaim. What's more, people seemed to react viscerally to it, and even, to John's surprise, to buy it.

It had been slow going, and he was already forty-four when this, his first book of prose, was published, and years of difficulty were still ahead. But thanks to a single struggling fish, John Hay had begun to make his name.

Later in the month I took John for a drive to the other end of Stony Brook, the mouth of Paine's Creek. He was feeling sick and listless, and the day was unseasonably cold, so we didn't even get out of the car. But I pointed the Civic toward the beach and rolled down the windows a bit, despite the chill. It was like watching a movie of the beach, something John would have disdained in his younger days or even last fall, but better than being cooped up at home. Birds shot every which way, and the wind blew swarms of sand along the shore. The running of the herring wasn't a boon for humans only, and a few hundred gulls gathered near the creek's mouth, awaiting the tide's change and the inrush of fish.

John looked out quietly, and it appeared that the effort of con-versation was beyond him. I was happy just to watch the show.

"Perhaps we'll see a tern or two," he eventually said, in a near whisper.

We didn't, but the expectation kept us watching longer than we might have.

In some ways, this stream that changed names and that, through a kind of alchemy, also changed from salt water to fresh, was an unre-markable body of water, "only a minor inlet," as John admitted. It was a creek or brook, not even a river, and you could easily jump across it at many points. But this modest body of water had originally brought the native peoples to the valley they would name after it, Sauquatuck-ett. And this brook brought the European settlers in to drive out the natives.

For John, the little brook was not just a great repository of life but a constantly replenishing inspiration. If the fish were the star of his first book, then the creek the fish swam in provided him with an inexhaustible source. In fact, for John, this two-mile-long stretch of shallow water had proven only a little less fertile than the Tigris and Euphrates. It was beside Paine's Creek, appropriately, that his Museum of Natural History, his center of human community, was built. And it was here that John had begun to develop a sense of responsibility and reciprocity between himself and the places he loved. Over the years he had tried to repay the little creek for what it had given him. For instance, he had been personally responsible for conserving all the marsh and woodland along it. At the same time the creek had given him so many things that he could never pay it back.

One of these things was a sense of being an intimate of communities other than human ones. Not just the herring: everything seemed to spring from this one place. Here John also encountered ruddy turnstones and black-crowned night herons and willets and turtles and muskrats and deer. And finally, it was here that he began to develop his deep bond with terns.

"I first started observing terns at the mouth of Paine's Creek," he had told me during a winter visit. "I was young, and obviously I didn't know much. I watched the young black-capped birds being fed by their parents. I thought it was fascinating. The more I watched their lives, the more I began to see them as living in communities. If you saw them as communities, you could get some sense of our human community and how it could be improved, not by wildlife but by wildness. It's the wildness that grabbed me."

Now, as we watched the ocean, I mentioned the way that this creek had tied him to the world. And to terns, one of the world's great migrators.

At first I wasn't sure that John had heard me. When he finally did reply, it was as if he were talking to himself. "Yes, it's true," he said. "This little creek led me to places I would have never expected.

As it turned out, I ended up following the terns halfway across the world, to Denmark and the coast of England and even Africa. But it all started here."

After I dropped off John on Dry Hill, I drove home and took a walk on the beach. As I headed out to the bluff that had become my own source, I thought about how perfect it was that so much of John's work had sprung from a small local stream. If what he called a "minor inlet" felt like a place entirely apart from the real world, it had proven again and again to be connected to other places all over that world. Both the herring and the terns, for instance, tied this one place to many places. The herring embarked on ambitious migrations, but after all their travels, they always returned to this stream, smelling their way back from the continental shelf and then nearly killing themselves with exhaustion trying to fight back home. The terns proved an even finer example of the connection between the local and the global. The birds underwent such preposterous feats of navigation, from pole to pole, that even scientists couldn't pretend to understand how they found their way.

"It struck me that these animals led magnificent, unexplored lives," John had said. "Take the terns, for instance. These birds may not be intelligent, by human standards, but they possess attributes we couldn't dream of. For one thing, they have a tremendous sense of timing. The trouble with our society is that it thinks that we are the ones who time everything. But when you get deeply involved in the natural world, you start to realize that everything is interconnected, and not only is it interconnected, but the timing is incredible. A tern that goes down to Antarctica every year and comes back at precisely the same time to the same nest! They never forget the spot where they last heard their parent's voice. This is a supposedly brainless bird? And how could any human dare do such a thing? So we say, 'Oh well, he's on automatic pilot'... all sorts of rationalizing about it, but the fact is these creatures have got minds. 'Bird brains' should be a compliment! They are enclosed by an environment that in a sense protects them and pushes them and energizes them, like the sun."

All types of terns, from common to royal to Forster's, fascinated John, but Arctic terns were particularly worthy of admiration, exemplifying his strangely cosmopolitan ruralism. Each year these small birds fly from the coast of Cape Cod toward Africa, just one short leg of their miraculous annual journey. After flying down the African coast, they circle the Antarctic polar cap before flying back up the coast of South America and through the United States and Canada to the place that gave them their name. Then they stay in the Arctic until fall, when they set out again, flying southeast across Canada to the beaches of Nova Scotia and Cape Cod, completing their global lap.

One characteristic of John's elastic mind has always been to yoke the global with the local. His passionate love affair with his own modest local place had, paradoxically, helped him to understand other places. Far from turning him into a bumpkin, as he'd feared, settling on Cape Cod had provided a solid foundation of home that let him venture outward in larger, speculative swings. As a younger man John flew after the terns, but just as important, he followed them in imagination, his thoughts taking equally grand and borderless flights. And it might not be going too far to say that by knowing his terns, he began to know the universe.

8

Exodus

With the warm weather came waves of movement. Not just the nestling ospreys breaking free of their eggs and the coyote pups spilling out of their dens, exploring the brackish world with their noses, or even the thousands of other creatures buzzing, croaking, and singing in the now green marshes, but human beings as well. The streets jammed, and houses that stood empty all winter suddenly filled. There was a massing, and a tension. In the course of a month the population of our little neighborhood would increase more than thirtyfold.

The people didn't come alone. They brought their cars with them. Cape Cod in summer has long acted as a magnet for automobiles; it was one of the first destinations of gas-powered vacations. In 1914 the Cape Cod Canal was completed, making this a true island, and then, in 1935, the two bridges over the canal opened. A year later more than 80,000 cars were pouring over those bridges on a "good" summer day. By 2001 that number had increased to 130,000, all of them traveling, as John Hay once put it, "to this narrow peninsula over the blistering, insatiable roads of America."

In May, John began to prepare for his annual migration to Maine. He always escaped Cape Cod right before it became cluttered with cars. The trip would be harder than in years past, with Kristi still sick and John himself growing weaker, but he was determined to stick to the cycle of their year. To give that up would be a sign of surrender.

One of the pleasures of the Maine house was that it sat right on the shore. "I think it would be best for Kristi to get up there and watch the water go by," he said to me one day. "Maybe the water will heal us."

I didn't mention that Nina and I were dealing with our own unsettling move. A couple of weeks before I had finally decided to take the teaching job and leave Cape Cod. In the end the decision was actually fairly easy. Nina was pregnant now, and things like health insurance and a salary were going to come in handy.

Samuel Johnson wrote about the "power of the last"—how when things near their end, they intensify. With only a few weeks left on the Cape, I tried to memorize the sights of beach and bluff and feel them in my blood so they would not go away. I listened to the crickets pulse in the dunes and watched the swallows swoop and dart in front of their cavelike homes. Each morning I walked out into the silver-edged world and stared at the crisp greens of budding trees and the great broiling of whitecaps on the bay. I wasn't ready to leave.

During those last weeks I was seized by last-second schemes. One of those schemes almost came to fruition. I was friends with both the owners of the house on the edge and the people who bought the place from them. The new owners planned to tear down the old house and build a new one. Therefore, neither the old nor the new owners had any use for the house we were living in. Together they decided to make Nina and me a startling offer: they would *give* us the house if we could find land to put it on! For a week I was in a fever. If I could only buy some land, I would have a home for my family. We would uproot the house we had grown to love and pull it by truck (or, better, by boat, across the bay) to new land. I ran around the Cape with a realtor, desperate, but it was the same old song. The prices for land were far beyond us.

Then I had one last crazy idea. What if I could talk John Hay into giving me a tiny piece of land at the base of Dry Hill, just as he had given Bob Finch his small plot many years before? Then I could transplant the edge house to Dry Hill. Why not? What could be a more fitting end for the house? But it was all too outrageous. Too desperate. I never even got up the nerve to mention it to John.

Finally the fever passed and I understood the simple truth. It was time to leave Cape Cod.

During those weeks I visited John often. One day he called me up, and when I drove over I found him waiting outside by the garden. Right away I noticed that his silver hair was now cut short, and I mentioned it. "Yes, I was looking a bit wild," he said.

He smiled but seemed distracted. He pointed at the cars in the driveway. "People all try to run your life when you get older," he lamented.

We wandered up to his study and I sat in my now familiar seat. I tried to describe an environmental clash that was occurring in our neighborhood, my latest run-in with the owner of the trophy house next door, but John seemed distracted. One of the things I had hoped to do before I left was to try to take him on a kayak trip up Stony Brook, but now I saw that this wasn't going to happen. The brief resurgence of energy he had felt in April had faded. The only time he seemed truly comfortable was when he drifted into the far past, telling old stories as if they had happened yesterday.

As usual, he was better once we got outside. In the garden he was delighted by the azure butterflies that landed on flowers the same color as they were. When the butterflies closed their wings, the blue disappeared, swallowed up by their drab brown outer wings.

John studied the big cherry tree for a while. Its blossoms now looked shriveled. "The early warming isn't good for it," he said. "It's not good for herring, either. Or for humans, for that matter."

We took a short walk down the driveway, and he pointed out the lichen on the base of the oaks—"Look how it seems to come alive after the rain"—and then the rhododendrons he had planted forty years before, which now lined the road. "It's always been a good place for deer down there," he said, gesturing toward a gully off in the woods.

Farther down the road, he jabbed his cane toward two robins. "'A

caucus of robins in an alien spring,' " he recited. He turned his suddenly alert gaze on me. "You know who said that?"

I admitted I didn't.

"Conrad Aiken."

Aiken, as usual, proved an immediate portal to the living past.
"Robert Lowell used to visit Conrad," John said. "There was something about Lowell that scared me a little. Conrad liked him because
he dressed so well, but what was inside him wasn't well. He always tried
to pry inside your head. Always tried to get a rise out of you. 'Why are
you so facetious all the time?' he asked me. He liked to prod and prick."

He interrupted his story to smell a small plant growing along one
of the banks at the side of the road. "Trailing arbutus," he explained.
"They call it mayflower around here. No relation to the English mayflower. It grows along old disturbed roads."

I looked at the little white flower from a few feet away, as if examining a museum painting. John laughed at me.

"Stick your nose in there and smell it!" he said. "That's how you
get to know it. That's how you introduce yourself to flowers. Introduce
yourself, for god's sake!"

I did as I was told, sucking in the sweet smell.

"Pick some, if you like, and take it home to your wife," he added.
"She'll love the smell."

We stood still for a while and listened to the trees swaying in the
wind. Though it seemed as if we'd undertaken a significant journey,
we had really walked only about a hundred yards down the driveway.

Now John started climbing a path that cut back up the hill to the study. His property was threaded with these paths, like deer paths, paths he'd explored for years, though some were no longer accessible to him. Considering that he wasn't walking well, I was surprised he had chosen this steep ascent.

"It's like mountain climbing," I said.

"The last time I tried real mountain climbing, it didn't go that well, I'm afraid. I was eighty, and after climbing for an hour I had to give up."

He did better today. Then, just as we reached the clearing near the top of the path, a sharp, unearthly cry came from above. We looked up to catch a glimpse of a burly-chested red-tailed hawk through the tops of the pines, its burnished tail patch showing. John stared up, smiling long after the bird had left.

"Do you know the Hopkins line?" he asked.

I shook my head.

" 'My heart in hiding stirred for a bird,—the achieve of; the mastery of the thing!' " As he shuffled back to the studio, he quietly repeated the phrase "stirred for a bird."

We reclaimed the same seats in the studio, but John seemed revived by the walk. I decided to take the opportunity to ask him about religion again. I had questioned him about it some during the year but wasn't satisfied with his answers.

Bob Finch had said that John's lifework had been an "essentially poetic enterprise," but it had also been an essentially spiritual one. When I mentioned this idea to John, he agreed.

"That's a reasonable assumption," he said. "Because I don't think everything can be explained by an agnostic, mechanical world."

I nudged him on, asking about the connection between the natural and the spiritual.

"The modern world often sees nature as just another commodity," he said. "They see it in terms of what is useful to them. But they don't see it as something that causes wonder. Or, to use a fine word that my friend Eric Levy uses, *wonderment*. They don't understand that there is something more important in a tree than they know. It's hard to follow nature if you don't believe in continual discovery. If you think you know it all already. People don't know about nature unless they get down in it. Down in the water and the dirt."

I still wasn't satisfied. "Do you believe in God?" I asked bluntly.

"I don't like the question much. Too *either-or*. I believe in gods." He let that answer sit for a second before correcting himself. "No, that's not it exactly either. I believe that there is more than we can understand. I believe in the mystery. And in the ritual and ceremony that connect us to the mystery. Without these, we are dead."

After a moment he leaned toward me and spoke more emphatically. He gestured forward with his hand, as if this were something he needed to say.

"That's the crux of the problem. Nature provides the mystery, and we are destroying nature. As is often the case, humans don't know what the hell they're doing. Destroying the thing that gives them life. The fount. Environmental issues, as they are called, seem abstract to most people. But they are the opposite of abstract. They are *life*." He shook his head. "Nature—the mystery—never lets us down. But we let it down all the time. All life is ceremony, and when you destroy ceremony, you destroy life itself."

We said goodbye soon after, John walking me down to my car and waving from the lawn as I drove off.

On the way home I thought that if John was raging against anything, it wasn't death. Cessation was acceptable; what wasn't was a gradual dulling. "I want to feel raw life, raw as a codfish pulled out of the cold sea…" But for John, life was less and less often codfish-raw. He would never again feel his full strength flow back into him.

One afternoon when Nina and I were doing the final cleaning of the rental house, we found ourselves vacuuming out a little nook with a child's bed built into the wall. It was a quirky bit of architecture, and we wondered which of the owner's kids had slept there, with its view of the bay, and what memories they must have attached to it. A week later all the family furniture was tagged for an estate sale. I couldn't help but feel that what was happening in this particular house—this beautiful house on the edge of the sea—was what was happening to the entire peninsula, maybe the entire country. The old was being torn down for the new, tradition and heritage tossed aside as if they were just another thing we could do without.

It was more complicated than that, of course; it always is. I happened to respect the family who had bought the place, but at the same time I wondered if they would know just what they had in it. Would they appreciate the bluff's moods? Would they understand the uncertain stability the place provided? Would they know to search for the coyote skull I had hidden in the rocks below the bluff? The new owners were good people, but we already knew that they planned to follow the recent pattern, and by tearing down the old house on the property, they would be tearing down a part of the past.

I couldn't help but feel that the former owners, being human, didn't yet understand how much they would miss the house. I already suspected how much I would miss it.

"It's good you're getting away from here," John said to me one day. "If I were young, I'd strike out for someplace new. This is a dying place."

He was right, of course. Anyone could see that Cape Cod had become something else, something different from what it had been. It had always been a summer playground for the rich, but it had also always had its secret self, its winter self. Now summer had spilled over into the rest of the year. Long gone were the days when you could, as John told me, walk down the middle of Route 6A to the post office. Though you might still be able to find hidden places, like the osprey nest out on the marsh, the old frontier feel was missing.

I knew all this, and I knew John was right, but I still couldn't quite convince myself that I was doing the right thing. And though I told myself that Cape Cod was ruined, I couldn't pretend that leaving would be easy. The ocean—which had drawn John here in the first place— still held me like a magnet. While I knew I was overdoing the melodrama, on some level I believed I was making myself an exile. And there was also something in the way of surrender, of relinquishment, in what I was doing. Not death, of course, but a small death. I was giving up not just the place but the idea that I would forever commit to a place on earth.

John and Kristi would move away for the summer, but their migration had a regularity of time and place that could make even change feel consistent. As usual, they would leave Cape Cod around summer solstice and wouldn't set foot back on the Cape until the tourists cleared out in September. This had the advantage of missing the crowds but the disadvantage of not seeing the full turn of the seasons in one place. But the trip to Maine had become as natural as breathing, and marked a part of their year as surely as the migrations of the terns and herring did. Animals, John had learned, were sparked to migrate by the slant of the sun, secreting hormones in accordance with the sunlight's angle and strength as it came in through the eyes, and his own annual migration wasn't so different. When the light got to a certain point in the sky, it was time to go.

The morning they left, I visited John and Kristi to say goodbye. With the solstice nearing, the driveway was canopied with the vibrant green of oak leaves. It was a warm, drizzly day, and honeysuckle and Scotch broom added to the lushness. I drove over unannounced and found John amid stacks of boxes piled up all around the house.

Deborah Diamond and a friend were going to drive the Hays to

Maine. John began to explain again why they were making the trip, though I hadn't asked. He sounded as if he were trying to convince himself, which was understandable. For two people near ninety, one very sick, a five-hundred-mile move was not an easy thing.

"I need to get back to where there's some space," he said to me. "The space is gone on Cape Cod."

I thought about how the word *space* had seemed somewhat vague and nondescriptive during our first meeting. Now I understood that it was synonymous with freedom. And I had begun to see that it was also connected, in ways less than entirely rational, to creativity and wildness.

John decided he needed a break from packing, and we walked up to the studio, which was barely visible amid the camouflage of birch and red and white oaks. I thought of a Mayan word for intense, verdant green—*yax*—that I had learned in Belize. The day was so alive that we decided to make a detour on the way to the studio, then decided not to go into the studio at all. Instead we walked out back behind the house, where many years before John had planted a wild garden of rhododendron and laurel. We walked through a tunnel of rhododendron, the leaves wet and green.

"I should have brought my machete," I said.

"My father kept his around the house," he said. "For his work down in Mexico." He pointed to a huge rhododendron called 'Maximus.' "I brought the rhododendron down from Maine maybe ten years ago. The rest of the stuff I planted from seed. The seed was very fine, like cinnamon."

The laurel was just beginning to bloom a whitish pink. "It will blossom full pink," he explained.

The path wove through the trees, by a beautiful beech tree. "I suppose I was trying to create the feel of a public garden. Like my father did in New Hampshire."

After our walk, we rested and drank lemonade on the porch. I told him I was anxious about leaving Cape Cod.

"The Cape isn't a place for permanence," he said reassuringly. "It's just a fragile land that briefly rose out of the sea. It's only a matter of time until the water takes it again. Until it sinks into the sea."

"But it's not going to sink in the next few years," I said.

"No." He laughed, and then turned serious. "But remember that you can always make something new. Cape Cod is not just Cape Cod. Cape Cod is any place and every place."

Though this was vague, I thought I understood what he meant. Cape Cod was just Cape Cod the way Walden Pond was Walden Pond, both any pond and every pond.

But then he laughed again. "On the other hand, Cape Cod is very much Cape Cod. This land is only this land. Individual and particular. Surrounded and blessed by the sea."

I wished him a safe trip to Maine. Then I walked back and climbed into my car. I held my hand out the car window and waved as I started down the long driveway. It felt strange, and uncomfortable, to be leaving Dry Hill and not coming back.

There was a deeper leaving, too. In the course of my year of visits, I felt like I had witnessed the passing of something. Just as John had seen the last subsistence farmers on the Cape, I was confident that in John I was seeing the last of his kind. For one thing, no one was going to stroll into Brewster and buy fifty acres of wooded hilltop, and if someone did, you could be sure it wouldn't stay wooded long before a giant condo was planted atop it. At least the land on Dry Hill would be preserved, a much-trammeled but wild place that would only grow wilder in years to come. But John himself would be gone soon, and, as he had said of Aiken, "He's the type that's gone out." Something final would pass out of the world when he left.

Before I had walked to my car, John had said that he hoped I'd enjoy my new home and my new explorations. I told him that I wanted to visit him again at some point to record more of his stories.

"I'll try and stay alive until then," he said as we shook hands. "That will be my part."

EPILOGUE

The Prophet Down the Road

I left Cape Cod. I now live a thousand miles to the south, and having been here a while, I suspect I will stay. But if I have undergone
a sea change, I still live by the same sea. During an exploratory visit
to our new home, I found the perfect house, off a dirt path in the
woods. But then, just as I was about to sign the lease, something else
came up—a rental on the small barrier island over the drawbridge outside of town. On impulse, my wife and I decided to take it, in no small
part because we could see the water through the dining room window.

At first the move unsettled me. I felt—to use an overused metaphor—pulled out by the roots. During those shaky early days, I tried
to write the story of my year with John Hay, but I wasn't ready yet. It
took two seasons in my new home before I could begin to put John in
the past tense. By then I'd long known that it wasn't a biography I was
after but a simple record of our days together. Still, I felt some trepidation about writing about John.

On one level, having spent so much time thinking about John's chronicling of Cape Cod, the prospect of writing about the Cape again also seemed intimidating. I procrastinated in various ways, turning to other projects, but one day I got some consolation for my anxiety from an unexpected source. That afternoon I took a walk along my new beach and watched pelicans dive, twisting down into the water, following their divining-rod bills. When I got home, I happened to pick up a book I had bought at Parnassus long before, a thin volume by Conrad Aiken called *Sheepfold Hill,* signed by Aiken in 1969. I opened it at random and found myself reading from the poem "Mayflower."

Learning the literary history of Cape Cod had been a generally pleasurable experience, but I still had some reservations. In a culture that prizes "originality" above all else, the traditional becomes suspect. Wasn't it dangerous for a writer to be spending so much time so close to another writer? What about the dreaded "anxiety of influence"? Weren't writers supposed to kill their literary forefathers? My own adventures in nature had always felt original to me, but the more I read John's work, the more I saw he had often been there first. Wasn't I wasting too much time going over old ground? These were legitimate worries, and I would think about them more in the months to come, as I began to write. But the truth was that they quickly disappeared when I opened the old book and the musty smell rose off the faded pages. The poems seemed much more accessible than those of Aiken's I'd read before. I read with a high degree of enjoyment, and that enjoyment intensified and personalized when I read these lines:

Lost, lost, lost, lost—the bells from Quivett Neck
sing through the sabbath fog over ruin and weeds.

Quivett Neck, home of Crowes Pasture, was right across the harbor from where we had lived on Cape Cod. During my year visiting John, I had heard those same Quivett bells from the old church morning and night, ringing over the water.

Soon I was entirely absorbed in the poetry. I read about time and timelessness:

Three hundred years: in time's eye only a moment.
Time only for the catbird's wail,
from one June to another, flaunting his tail,
the joyful celebrant with his own mournful comment.

Time only for a single dream,
as, in this misty morning, all our generations seem,
seem only one, one face, one hope, one name:
those who first crossed the sea, first came,
and the newborn grandchild, crying, one and the same.
Yes now, now most of all, in fateful glare
of mankind's hatred everywhere,
time yields its place, with its own bell
uncharms and then recharms its spell:
and time is gone but everything is here,

all is clear, all is one day, one year,

the many generations seem,

and are, one single purpose, one single name and dream.

Three hundred years from Will and Ben

our country's clock wound up again.

I put the book down and thought about the way past merges with future and present with past. *Three hundred years: in time's eye only a moment.* Different generations of catbirds but the same species, still singing each spring. And different generations of human beings, too, of course, living in a place and responding to it just as they always had. With words and sentences. Singing the land.

I experienced a brief, strange sensation. Though it sounds silly, I felt a little like I was communicating with a ghost. Of course Aiken hadn't achieved any real sort of immortality; he was moldering both in the ground and in the libraries. But if he had no literary immortality, then what did exist for him was what Keats called "immortal freemasonry," the possibility of communication between writers and readers of different time periods. I was alive, and Aiken could still communicate with me, and I back to him, though he wouldn't hear me. Whatever the case, a chill ran through me. I experienced a fleeting wordless pleasure and then, after a few seconds, put words to it. I felt, however briefly, not so much an individual as a part of a larger tradition. And part of a lineage. I was left feeling less alone. And less nervous. This idea had occurred to me before, but now it struck with great force: the job of celebrating Cape Cod, or any individual place, was not any one person's job. It was the work of generations.

This past spring I returned to Cape Cod, though this time I returned on vacation, as a visitor, with no illusions that I would settle there. On my second day back I drove up the long winding driveway to Dry Hill with my daughter, Hadley, in her car seat. We got out of the car and she rode my shoulders as I walked around the place. At first I thought to myself that it probably didn't look that different from when John had moved here in 1946. But then I stared up at the swaying trees and realized how much those trees had changed the character of the stunted landscape that John had first found. Over the years he had watched his hill reforest itself, like watching a bald man sprouting hair.

It looked just as I remembered it, though. The gardens were still tended, and the place was lush with spring green. No doubt the herring were running down at Stony Brook and the peepers were singing. The world was in place.

There was a difference, however. Though the property looked the same, its long-time occupants were missing. For the first spring in almost sixty years John Hay wasn't tramping the trails over Dry Hill. As it turned out, the Hays had found Maine to their liking. For one thing, they liked the health care better—the nurses were "less intrusive,"

John told me on the phone—and in Maine they were closer to their children, two of whom lived relatively nearby. Just as important, in Maine John felt less confined, felt that he had more space. And so after the summer passed they made a startling choice. Rather than return to the Cape, as they had every fall for so many years, they decided to stay in Maine. Strange, that the person who had saved more land than any other on Cape Cod and who had chronicled the Cape for so long no longer lived there. In the end he had become unsettled. If John's pastoral adventure had had a longer duration than most, it too had been temporary. Like Thoreau, John had other lives to live. His house-ship had become unmoored and drifted across the bay, heading north.

Dry Hill sat abandoned. No one was around, and I'll admit that I wasn't shy about exploring the property. I didn't enter the house, but I did take Hadley on a tour of the woods, the rhododendrons, the path up to the studio. I showed it to her as if it were something personal, something of my own, and I even let her peek inside the studio at the picture of Whitman and the now unused desk. Manuscripts still spilled from the closet, and cobwebs spanned the magnifier. I closed the door and decided it would be fun to try to take my daughter down to listen to the spring peepers at Berry's Hole. We walked the acorn-littered driveway and started hiking down toward that watery bowl with its singing frogs. But we soon retreated—the hill was too steep for me to carry a child.

I was surprised, in a guilty way, to see a car coming up the drive-way. It turned out to be the Hays' gardener, Jess, which explained why the grounds were still in decent shape. I introduced myself and we talked for a while. Then I put Hadley back in the car and headed off, making my last trip ever down Dry Hill. As I drove away, I thought about what I'd learned on that hill, what I had taken from the place. And I tried to think about John's legacy. What he had left behind there.

If you were to suggest to the fishermen and carpenters who lived down the street from John Hay that he was one of the great artists and original thinkers of the latter part of the twentieth century, you could forgive them if they rolled their eyes. The old guy in the baseball cap, baggy khakis, and flannel shirt who grumbled about traffic and tourists hadn't exactly looked the part of environmental prophet. Just another salty Cape Cod crank.

Still, while he lived on Dry Hill, more than a few neighbors penetrated his disguise. During my conversation with Jess, he offhandedly mentioned John's work. "I didn't know he was a writer at first, and I'm glad," he said. "If I knew how brilliant he was, I wouldn't have been able to talk to him."

Jess's opinion is more or less in line with that of environmental critics. The editors of *The Norton Book of Nature Writing* call John Hay "one of the most innovative and daring of contemporary writers in the genre." James Dickey, the poet and the author of *Deliverance*, went a little further: "If all of humanity were to read Mr. Hay's work, it is not unlikely that Darwin and St. Francis of Assisi would come back and join hands."

No matter that the octogenarians who frequent the East Dennis post office, where John used to mail his packages, might frown at the sight of those two dead men holding hands, and no matter that not quite all of humanity has read John Hay's work. The point is that, unknown to most of his neighbors, the old man who lived up on Dry Hill played a significant role in the development of American environmental thought and literature. Henry David Thoreau, of course, was the fountainhead of this thought, and it would be hyperbolic to suggest that John was as original and germinative as his great predecessor. But John has both preserved and expanded Thoreauvian thought. He is both a radical and a traditionalist, going back to old ways, grounded ways, but simultaneously using empathy to throw himself into new worlds beyond the human.

And just as important, to me at least, John has lived a life that has kept time with a different sort of clock. A life in tune with more elemental movements and ritual, a life of ceremony. I now live on the edge of a city full of strip malls and southern accents. But I also still live on the edge of the ocean, in a place that, if not my home beach, is a beach nonetheless. It is in the ocean that I see possibilities and through the ocean that I can begin to imagine making a life here. Every day I try to get out to the edge of the sea, confident that this will change me in ways I can't quite put into words. In spring and fall I watch the migrations, hoping these movements will become part of me, part of my blood. I hope to follow the year's journey, absorbing its rhythms. I dream of living an elemental life.

Most often I fail.

But I try. And while the concept of learning from elders often seems hopelessly outdated, I am happy to have had an arrow-shooter, an exemplar, someone who walked out ahead to show me it can be done. Not a perfect character—hardly. But someone who made a journey out of his time on earth. Someone who tried, in his own words, to "go farther afield, from one man's center."

"People connect to the land as their imaginations allow," wrote William Least Heat-Moon. John's imagination allowed for no less than a lifelong, passionate love affair with the world. When I think of John now, with some distance, I no longer shy away from calling him a prophet. Granted, *prophecy* is a big word, a grand archaic word that understandably scares people off. But it is also, I've come to believe, the right word. Here is a man who had his vision and then spent his life trying to articulate that vision. Part of that articulation was attempting to convince people that the things they valued were not the things of greatest value, that a whole secret life was available to them if they only reordered their priorities. In this sense, John fit all three major definitions of a prophet: he had his divine vision, he was a leader of a movement, and he presented a vision of the future.

That vision—of cancerous development and growth, of the disregard for and uprooting of local people, animals, and places—was, like most prophetic visions, somewhat apocalyptic. This is nothing new. Apocalyptic language has always been a tool of the prophets, who describe the apocalypse in hopes of preventing it. "We create images of doom to avert doom," wrote Lawrence Buell; "that is the strategy of the jeremiad." Or, as E. B. White put it, "A seer a day keeps Armageddon away." Of course, foresight—that is, *vision*—is the prophet's first tool, and John began issuing warnings about the world before anyone knew what the hell ecology was. This half-blind old man saw clearly both where we had come from and where we were going, and he didn't like it one bit.

Like the biblical prophets, John Hay went to his hill to find his vision, and sure enough, certain universal truths were revealed to him on his mountaintop. And like the prophets, he had tried to deliver this unwavering vision to an often unbelieving and uninterested public. "In wildness is the preservation of the world," said Thoreau. John believed that the best human lives are those connected to wildness on an intimate and daily basis, and that this connection affects human lives in ways they can't understand or explain. Was it any surprise that wild animals had larger brains—and more creative responses to the world—than their domestic cousins?

John spent a lifetime fighting to both live inside and preserve that wildness, and it had often been a depressing fight. He had watched the things he loved about Cape Cod be defiled and watched the rest of the country head in the same direction. Though people paid lip service to loving nature, they just didn't seem to take its destruction personally enough. Worse, he had been consistently ignored and misunderstood, labeled impractical and airy and snobbish. This hurt, but it didn't stop him. He had, in fact, become more and more passionate in his belief in the wild.

Jeremiah, for one, knew the impossibility of trying to deliver a message of cataclysm in an affluent time and, like John, was often greeted with some variant of the question "What's the fuss?" Trying to describe just what the fuss was was central to John's lifework. Jeremiah was labeled a traitor, and no doubt some people these days would label John as un-American for his consistent belief that less is better than more. But even those not inclined to thinking in terms of the apocalypse can't help but see that something close to cataclysmic seems to be coming: worldwide extinctions, global warming, rampant habitat loss. To change any of that, John believed, we first have to enact the most rigorous transformation of all: changing our own minds.

John's ideas, I believe now, were, and *are*, subtly radical. Primary among these ideas, the one embedded everywhere in his work, is the notion that human beings may not be so central to the world after all. There are human consequences, of course, to seeing the world as more than human-centered. These involve radical shifts in what one values in this life. If what truly matters is respecting the earth and preserving the diversity of ecosystems, then it follows that traditional ways of seeing land for what one can "get" from it are discarded.

These ideas are, of course, antithetical to a culture that always keeps half an eye cocked toward the mirror, to people who spend their time primping and fixing their hair. For fifty years John insisted that we should be looking, not in the mirror, but out and through the window. By focusing always inward and seeing the outer world only through our own inner constructs, we keep the eyes prisoner to the brain. And, as it turns out, the brain is a lonely place. By never making the leap out of self, we are left isolated, cold, and blind. But ultimately, if we follow our better instincts, we can climb right through the window, and there—outside of ourselves—we will find things that will expand our definitions of ourselves.

Unlike most of us, John spent his days training himself to look outward. In fact, it is this outward focus, this still-active love affair with the world, not the self, that most defines John Hay.

"Strange to have come through the whole century and find that the most interesting thing is the birds," John said to me during our very first walk together. "Or maybe it's just that the human mind is more interesting when focusing on something other than itself."

In this insistence on looking outward, John Hay ran entirely against the prevailing culture. He didn't believe that salvation of the self was to be found within the self. In fact, he saw this proposition, one of our culture's central tenets, as essentially neurotic and crippling. "The answers to life can't be found by trying to solve things in our brains," he said, "but by stepping out of our brains entirely." We can expand ourselves only by looking outward, toward the source, toward the mystery, and by joining the ritual of the natural year we can join that mystery. The good news is that the reflections we see of ourselves in our beloved places will be clearer ones than the ones we see in a mirror. By focusing inward, without reference to the world, we make islands of ourselves, but by looking outward we reinvent and expand ourselves.

I came to John Hay to write a book about him, not to seek lessons. But if there is one thing I took with me from Dry Hill, it is this: inwardness only means so much. What we need to learn is to get out of our own way. Yes, inward tunneling counts for something and something important, but there is so much more outside. If we look for it, we will find that a whole world is waiting for us. And it is in that world that we, not seeking it, will find a sort of salvation.